The Sinopedia Series

China's History

The Sinopedia Series

Editorial Board

Chief Advisor: Wang Chen
Chief Conceptualiser: Wang Zhongwei
Executive Producer: Guo Changjian
Publisher: Li Xiangping
Chief Editor: Wu Wei

The Sinopedia Series

China's History

CAO DAWEI
SUN YANJING

CENGAGE Learning™

CHINA INTERCONTINENTAL PRESS

Australia • Brazil • Japan • Korea • Mexico • Singapore • Spain • United Kingdom • United States

CENGAGE Learning

China's History
Cao Dawei and Sun Yanjing

Publishing Director:
  Paul Tan

Editorial Manager:
  Yang Liping

Associate Development Editor:
  Tanmayee Bhatwadekar

Associate Development Editor:
  Joe Ng

Senior Product Director:
  Janet Lim

Product Managers:
  Kevin Joo
  Lee Hong Tan

Assistant Publishing Manager:
  Pauline Lim

Production Executive:
  Cindy Chai

Translators:
  Xiao Ying
  Li Li
  He Yunzhao

Copy Editor:
  Jane Lael

Cover Designer:
  Ong Lay Keng

Compositor:
  Integra Software Services, Pvt. Ltd.

© 2011 Cengage Learning Asia Pte Ltd
Original Chinese edition © 2010 China Intercontinental Press

ALL RIGHTS RESERVED. No part of this work covered by the copyright herein may be reproduced, transmitted, stored or used in any form or by any means graphic, electronic, or mechanical, including but not limited to photocopying, recording, scanning, digitalizing, taping, Web distribution, information networks, or information storage and retrieval systems, without the prior written permission of the publisher.

For permission to use material from this text or product, submit all requests online at
www.cengageasia.com/permissions
Further permissions questions can be emailed to
asia.permissionrequest@cengage.com

ISBN-13: 978-981-4319-78-2

ISBN-10: 981-4319-78-3

**Cengage Learning Asia Pte Ltd
5 Shenton Way #01-01**
UIC Building
Singapore 068808

Cengage Learning is a leading provider of customized learning solutions with office locations around the globe, including Singapore, the United Kingdom, Australia, Mexico, Brazil and Japan. Locate your local office at: **www.cengage.com/global**

Cengage Learning products are represented in Canada by Nelson Education, Ltd.

For product information, visit **www.cengageasia.com**

Printed in Singapore
1 2 3 4 5 12 11 10

Table of Contents

Preface vii

Chapter 1. The Origin of Chinese Culture   3

Chapter 2. The Xia, Shang, and Western Zhou Dynasties: Early States and Bronze Civilization   17

Chapter 3. The Spring and Autumn and Warring States Periods: States Contend for Power, Control, and Social Reform   31

Chapter 4. The Qin and Han Dynasties: Establishment and Development of a Great Unified Country   53

Chapter 5. The Wei, Jin, and Southern and Northern Dynasties: Regime Division and Ethnic Concentration   77

Chapter 6. The Sui and Tang Dynasties: A Prosperous and Open Age   95

Chapter 7. The Song and Yuan Dynasties: Cultural Collision and Fusion and Socioeconomic Advances   119

Chapter 8. The Ming and Qing Dynasties (before the Opium War): Prosperity of the Farming Civilization and Crisis before Modern Times   145

Chapter 9. The Decline and Struggle of Modern China   177

Chapter 10. The People's Republic of China: In Search of Socialist Modernization   189

Appendix. Chronological Table of the Chinese Dynasties   201

Index   203

Preface

One of the earliest civilizations in the world, China is the only ancient civilization in world history with no interruption. The Chinese people have inherited a common culture and history longer than have any other people on earth.

Separated from the western civilization by mountains, deserts, and oceans, China is geographically independent. Fertile farmlands, prairies, and coastal areas for fishing and trading are spread over a vast space.

China's territory is the third largest in the world today, and up until the modern age, it had always been the largest. Its population was one-third of the global total over a fairly long time in history.

Living in East Asia's northern temperate zone, China's ancestors nurtured an agrarian economy. They stepped into the threshold of civilization from a stable agricultural community, and their clan chiefs grew into a new ruling class. Thus, kindred ties and a state administrative system fused into an underlying social structure, resulting in a tradition that emphasizes inwardness, community, human relations, and centralized power.

Intensive cultivation marked with the use of iron tools developed in the Yellow and Yangtze river basins in ancient China, forging an individual farming economy, private land ownership, and tenant contractual relationships.

The natural economy-based centralism, boasting a highly centralized state power and a well-organized hierarchy, competently exercised jurisdiction over a large population across a vast territory via professional officials selected through imperial examinations, and created smooth and efficient road and communication networks.

The application of a single writing system via characters and the prevalence of Confucian philosophy and culture have exerted a profound influence on the homogeneity and cohesion of the Chinese civilization.

The world experienced significant changes during the Ming and Qing dynasties (1368–1911). Major European countries entered into the industrial age. The rise of capitalism threw the whole world into a vast maelstrom of commodity circulation. Western powers swarmed into other continents across the oceans and established colonies. China reached a new peak in its course of farming civilization and showed some signs of modernization. However, the emperors of the early Qing Dynasty (1644–1991) turned a blind eye to the historical trend and kept China from the outside world. They stubbornly promoted the farming system while discouraging the budding industrial civilization. Hence, the positions of China and the West were overwhelmingly reversed, leading to a meteoric decline of China in the midst of industrial civilization.

The First Opium War broke out from 1840 to 1842. Three score years from then on, China, invaded and insulted by western powers, was forced to ink a series of unequal treaties to cede territory and pay indemnities, and fell into a colonial and semi-colonial abyss.

The invasion brought severe tribulations to the Chinese people and accelerated the disintegration of the restrictive traditional natural economy, giving rise to national capitalists and working classes and reducing the bankrupted peasantry to semi-proletariats.

During the century-long modernization dating from the Opium War, the Chinese people constantly promoted the development of national industry through struggles against imperialism, feudalism, and capitalism. The Revolution of 1911 led by Dr. Sun Yat-sen overthrew the Qing Dynasty, and helped the spread of concepts such as democracy and republic. Next, the revolution guided by the Communist Party of China won the great victory of national independence and people's liberation.

October 1, 1949 witnessed the founding of the People's Republic of China, inaugurating a new era toward socialist modernization. The reform and opening-up policy with Chinese characteristics was implemented after 30 years of zigzagging exploration. The policy galvanized China's efforts to practice democracy and rule of law in the political field and established a socialist market-oriented economy, enabling the country to actively participate in international competition and cooperation in economy. All these are done to work toward an affluent, democratic, cultural, sustainable, and harmonious society.

Ancient China's Silk Road played an important role in promoting China's relations with the outside world. The introduction of China's three great inventions—paper, gunpowder, and compass—to the western world expedited the formation of the bourgeois society. Meanwhile, western culture's eastward penetration and the promotion of Marxism significantly influenced the course of Chinese history. Today, the Chinese nation, with its brand-new forward-looking philosophy of pursuing modernization and opening up to the outside world, has integrated itself into the global community and will contribute significantly to safeguarding world peace and stability.

This book traces the unique trajectory and sums up the distinct features of the Chinese civilization and attempts to unlock the secret behind the continuity of the Chinese nation over thousands of years.

軒轅黃帝像

Chapter 1
The Origin of Chinese Culture

Primitive Humans and Tribes

China, a country with the highest number of primitive human sites in the world, has not only preserved the most abundant materials related to the origin of human beings, but also has had a fairly complete evolutionary process without serious interruptions.

In the early Paleolithic Period (about 250,000 to 2 million years ago), China's ancient ancestors were scattered over a vast area that covers today's Yunnan, Sichuan, Shanxi, Shaanxi, Henan, Hebei, Jiangsu, Anhui, Hubei, Guizhou, Inner Mongolia, Liaoning, and Beijing. Several hundred sites of the late Paleolithic Period, dating to about 10,000 to 40,000 years ago, have been found across China.

The progression from Yuanmou Man to Peking Man and then to Upper Cave Man outlines the evolution of early humans in China. Yuanmou Man dates to 1.7 million years ago, and was named after Yuanmou, Yunnan, where their fossils, two teeth and some handmade stone instruments, were unearthed. Coal dust and burned bones were found in clay layers. Yuanmou Man fossils are believed to be the earliest human remains in the Chinese territory.

The sedimentation layer of the caveman site at Longgu Mountain, Zhoukoudian, Beijing, is over 40 meters deep. Archeological study shows that Peking Man started to live in Zhoukoudian about 700,000 years ago and lived there for about 500,000 years. More than 17,000 pieces of stoneware, including choppers, scrapers, and arrowheads, were unearthed from the area. The six-meter-thick

The restored head portrait of Peking Man.

ash layer is evidence of Peking Man's ability to use fire for warmth, to cook food, give light, and drive away beasts. Peking Man, while retaining some physical features of apes, walked upright and had a brain capacity much higher than the ape's, about 76 percent of that of modern humans.

Remains of the Upper Cave Man were found in caves at the top of Longgu Mountain. Three pieces of human skull bones and some skeleton fossils; bone needles created by scratching, cutting, grinding, and drilling; pierced stone pearls, clam shells, and beast tusks; and other adornments were unearthed at the site. These indicate that the Upper Cave Man, who lived about 18,000 years ago, had mastered

Burned bones unearthed in the Peking Man Site indicate mastery of fire.

Chapter 1 The Origin of Chinese Culture

the skill of drilling wood to make fire. Manmade fire is deemed the beginning of human history. Upper Cave Man had nearly the equivalent brain capacity of modern human beings, as well as a similar physique and appearance.

About 10,000 years ago, the Chinese ancestors entered into the Neolithic Period. More than 7,000 sites, centered in the valleys of the Yangtze and Yellow rivers, are spread over a vast area. The Banpo Site of the Yangshao Culture (5,000 to 7,000 years ago) and the Hemudu Site of the Hemudu Culture (5,300 to 7,000 years ago) are representative of the early Neolithic Period, while the Longshan site (4,000 to 4,500 years ago) is typical of the late Neolithic Period.

The Banpo Site in the Yellow River basin, located in the Banpo village of Xi'an, Shaanxi, dates back 6,000 years and covers an area of about 50,000 square meters. The Banpo people lived in half-buried caves built with wood, branches,

The restored head portrait of Upper Cave Man.

or grass, and each had a stove made of clay and a *kang*, a fire-warmed brick sleeping platform. More than 200 silos used to preserve food were found. Tools and bones were excavated from the site, as were colorful porcelains with geometric patterns and human and animal designs.

The 7,000-year-old Hemudu Site in Hemudu Village, Yuyao, Zhejiang, is typical of the Yangtze River basin settlements, whose stilt style of architecture has for thousands of years been a major architectural form used in areas south of the Yangtze.

In the Neolithic Period, the ancient people widely used stone-made axes, spades, hoes, knives, millstones, and other ground-stone tools. They planted millet, rice, cabbage, mustard, and other crops, and raised pigs, dogs, oxen, goats, chickens, and other livestock.

The Xi'an Banpo Site and the Lintong Jiangzhai Site of the Yangshao Culture both have a central communal activity area surrounded by small residential rooms. Kilns for baking pottery were located near the residential quarters. A moat for protection was excavated around the village, and its tombs lie beyond the moat. The Niuheliang Site of the Hongshan Culture has a temple for worshipping a goddess and a large altar. These sites indicate the existence of a clan,

6 CHINA'S HISTORY

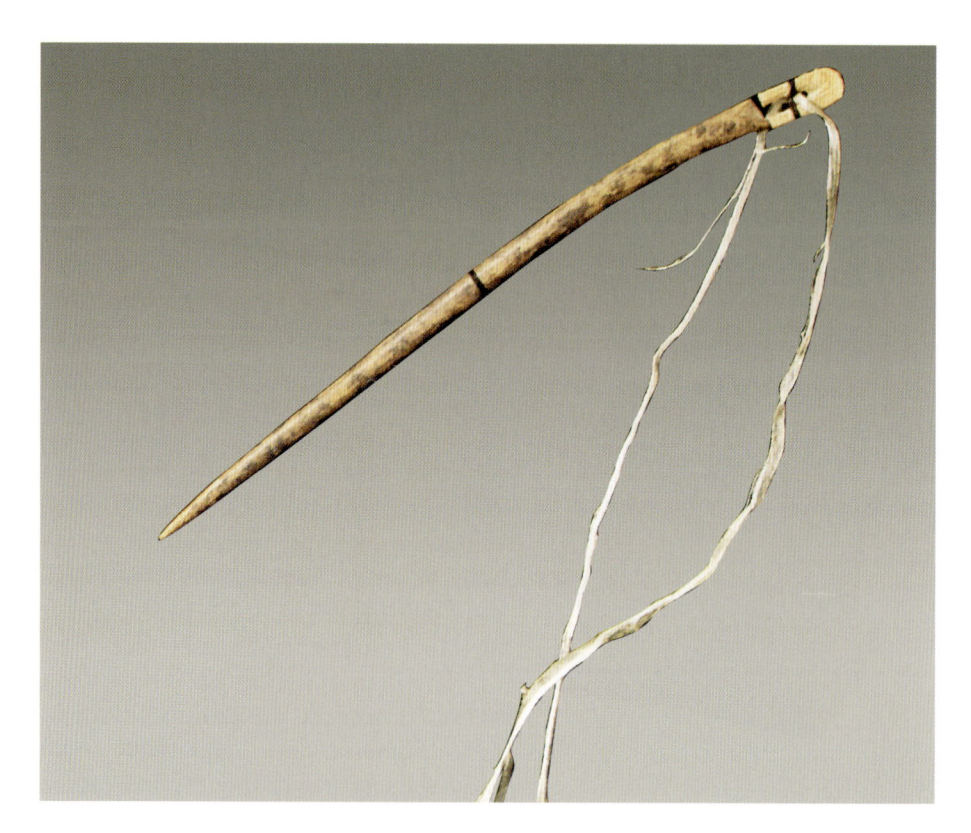

Bone needles and adornments made by Upper Cave Man.

Chapter 1 The Origin of Chinese Culture 7

Rice unearthed at the Hemudu Culture Site, Yuyao County, Zhejiang.

Pig-pattern black pottery bowl unearthed at the Hemudu Culture Site, Yuyao County, Zhejiang

Grinding stones of the Neolithic Age, unearthed in Peiligang, Xinzheng County, Henan.

Clay mask of an earthen goddess of the Hongshan Culture period, unearthed at Niuheliang, Liaoning.

An altar at the Hongshan Culture Site, Niuheliang, Liaoning.

a kinship-based community with families as the basic units. A tribe normally consisted of a few clans.

The progression from being hunter-gatherers to doing primitive agriculture and livestock husbandry, as well as the resulting settlements and clan society are all signs of increased productivity brought about by profound changes in mode of production and social structure.

Glimmer of Civilization in Legendary Times

Around 3,000 BC, the Tigris and Euphrates valleys in West Asia and Egypt in Africa entered the threshold of civilization, as did the Yellow River Valley and the middle and lower reaches of the Yangtze River in China. The history of remote antiquity was passed down mainly through oral myths and legends, and later was recorded in written documents.

Huangdi (Yellow Emperor) and Yandi (Flame Emperor) were the chieftains of tribal groups along the Yellow River some 4,000 to 5,000 years ago. Later generations, in their efforts to enumerate their ancestors' feats, attributed key inventions to these two leaders.

The Portrait of Huangdi (rubbing from the stone sculpture of the Han Dynasty at Wu's Memorial Temple in Jiaxiang, Shandong).

  Yandi, also known as Shennong Shi, the legendary founder of primitive agriculture and medicine, is said to have invented pottery and established markets for exchange. Huangdi, also known as Xuanyuan Shi, invented bows, arrows, and vehicles, and taught people sewing and building. He ordered his subordinates to invent characters, the calendar, arithmetic, and music. His

Chapter 1 The Origin of Chinese Culture   11

The Mausoleum of Huangdi at Huangling County, Shaanxi, is a place where his descendants burn incense in his honor.

Bone flutes of the Neolithic Age, unearthed at Jiahu, Wuyang County, Henan.

wife, Lei Zu, created the skill set of planting mulberry, raising silkworms, and weaving brocade with the silk produced.

The extant tombs and cultural relics of the Neolithic Period (4,000 to 8,000 years ago) provide evidence for these legends. Silkworm cocoons and spinning wheels unearthed in Xiaxian County, Shanxi, prove that sericulture and textiles were popular at the time. Colored earthen kettles in the shape of ships unearthed at the Banpo Site are indicators of shipbuilding. Symbols discovered at Banpo and other sites show the rudiments of written characters. Clay *xun* (globular flute) excavated in Banpo and bone flutes in Wuyang, Henan, testifies to the existence of musical instruments in the Neolithic period.

Unearthed in Banpo, pottery *zeng*, pots with a hole at the bottom, show that people steam-cooked their food. The house layout and pottery patterns illustrate arithmetic progression and symmetric design. The number symbols of I, II, III, X, 人, 十 (ten),

Boat-shaped painted pottery kettles of the Yangshao Culture period, unearthed at Beishouling, Baoji, Shaanxi.

and 八 (eight) engraved on pottery unearthed at Wuyang, Henan, are the same in meaning as those of later inscriptions on bones and tortoise shells. Some bone flutes still have the half-line mark for drilling holes, indicating accurate calculation.

These inventions, key elements that advanced the Chinese ancestors into the age of civilization, are the root source of many later great achievements. Huangdi and Yandi, therefore, are respected as the first ancestors of the Chinese people.

The Huangdi and Yandi tribes, originating from the Loess Plateau in northern Shaanxi, continued to expand eastward along the Yellow River. Together,

A painted pottery basin of the Neolithic Age, unearthed at the Banpo Site, Shaanxi. The decorative pattern features a human face with two fish in its mouth.

Chapter 1   The Origin of Chinese Culture   13

they defeated the Chiyou Tribe in the river's lower reaches. Later, Huangdi defeated the Yandi in the Banquan campaign to capture the central plains, gradually achieving the integration of the Yandi, Huangdi, and Chiyou tribes, creating the main population base of the Chinese nation.

Dragon images were discovered in Puyang, Henan, in tombs that date back 6,000 years. The dragon image was formed by integrating the totems of many tribes, reflecting their progression from conducting inter-tribal wars to forging alliances that led to the formation of the majority population of the Chinese people.

In the late Neolithic Period, productivity increased rapidly. Bronze artifacts unearthed in Gansu, Qinghai, and other places indicate that bronze and stoneware were both used in this period, about 4,000 years ago. More than 100 pieces of pottery and jadeware were found in tombs of this era.

The heroes of this period are Yao, Shun, and Yu, famous chieftains of the Yellow River valley tribes who ruled after Yandi and Huangdi. The area suffered severe floods during the times of Yao and Shun. Yu directed the people to dredge the rivers,

A human-shaped pottery pot of the Neolithic Age, unearthed at Dadiwan, Qin'an, Gansu.

A dragon laid with conches unearthed from a tomb at Puyang, Henan. It is honored as the "First Dragon in China."

The stone carving of Yu's water control project at Yuwangtai, Kaifeng.

FYI — FOR YOUR INFORMATION

FEATURES OF CHINA'S PRIMITIVE AGRICULTURE

Agriculture originated from three regions in the world: West Asia, East Asia, and Central and South America. The agricultural center of East Asia is China, whose agriculture dates back some 10,000 years and became well developed 7,000 to 8,000 years ago.

China's primitive agriculture and animal husbandry had distinctive features when compared to the rest of the world. In China, millet dominated in the North and rice in the South; in West Asia, wheat and barley were the major crops. Central and South America grew mainly potatoes and corn. In terms of animal husbandry, dogs, pigs, chickens, and water buffalo were among those first raised in China. The list later expanded to include three more domestic animals— horses, cattle, and sheep. Sheep and goats were dominant in West Asia, and alpacas were the only livestock raised in Central and South America.

and after thirteen years of hard work, the disasters were finally brought under control. He also led the people to build irrigation projects. Agricultural production in the Central Plains developed rapidly and Yu's influence extended to the Yangtze and Huaihe river basins.

According to historical records, Yu set up nine prefectures, built new roads, controlled nine lakes, and removed numerous mountains. This helped break tribal boundaries and integrate various tribes into a unified social community. Yu also gave instructions on production based on the geological features of different regions, asked the regions to pay tributes, and distributed grain among the regions to maintain an overall balance. Yu's extraordinary capabilities and enormous achievements helped him establish authority over the whole region.

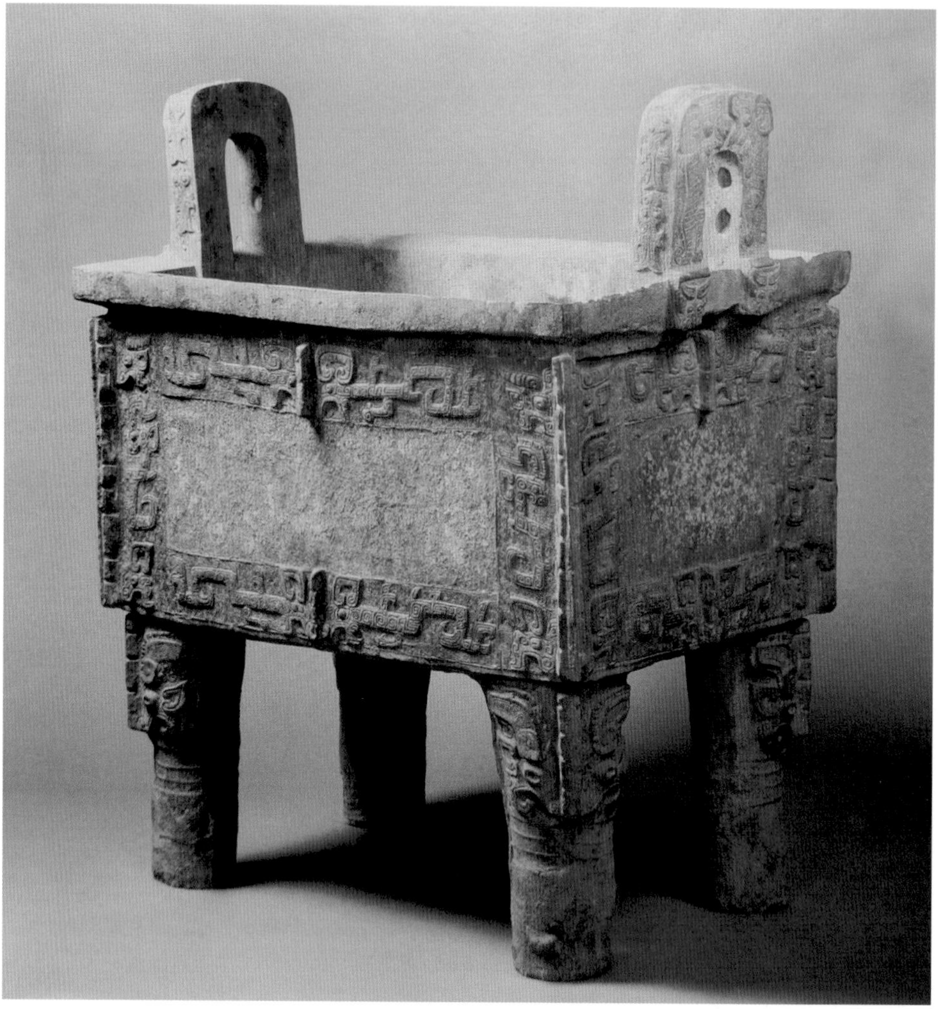

Chapter 2

The Xia, Shang, and Western Zhou Dynasties: Early States and Bronze Civilization

Presence of the State and Change of Dynasties

The Xia, Shang, and Western Zhou dynasties were an important period for the formation and development of early states.

Around 2070 BC, Yu set up Xia, the first dynasty in Chinese history. Yu divided the whole country into nine regions and established the capital in Yangcheng (today's Dengfeng). The administrative regions included today's Henan, Hebei, Shanxi, Shandong, Shaanxi, Jiangsu, Zhejiang, Anhui, Hubei, and so on. Yu also collected all the bronze in the state to make nine huge *Dings* (ancient cooking vessels), symbols of supreme authority.

The Xia Dynasty built palaces and cities with walls and moats for protection, established management institutions for different matters, and set up official posts at different levels. Furthermore, it also defined tributes and taxes, set up military forces, created rituals and criminal laws, built jails, and carried out other functions of a sovereign state.

The succession of authority from Yao and Shun to Yu was originally performed through peaceful abdication of power. Yu, by means of his authority, used his son Qi's power to defeat the Dongyi Tribe Chieftain Yi, the planned successor of Yu, and conquered other rebellious tribes. From then on, the hereditary system replaced the abdication system, a practice followed in later dynasties.

While there are few historical records of the Xia Dynasty, archeological excavations complement the historical records, presenting a relatively complete cultural view of the dynasty.

The area and period of existence suggested by the Erlitou cultural relics from Yanshi, Henan, generally match the location of the Xia Dynasty. At the site, the earliest palace cluster discovered in China to date was discovered. Standard and orderly in layout, symmetrical along the central line, it was equipped with roads and pottery-pipe ditches, and had a temple for offering sacrifices to ancestors. Jade, pottery, and bronze ritual ware were excavated at the site. Cast bronze and pottery mills were distributed around the city, indicating a social division of labor. The difference in tomb systems and funereal articles, and the more than thirty skeletons with signs of binding and execution, were indicative of the era's social hierarchy. All indicate the establishment of the rudiments of a country in the Xia Dynasty.

The Xia Dynasty lasted more than 470 years. The final ruler of the Xia, being cruel and extravagant, was opposed by the masses and deserted by his followers. Around 1600 BC, Tang, the chieftain of the Shang Tribe that lived in the lower reaches of the Yellow River, united numerous tribes to terminate the Xia Dynasty and establish the Shang Dynasty with Bo as its capital (Yanshi, Henan). The capital was later relocated several times. In 1300 BC, Pangeng, ruler of the Shang, moved the capital to Yin (today's Anyang, Henan), where the dynasty regime stayed till its end. Thus, the Shang Dynasty, the first documented era of China, is also called the Yin Dynasty. The Shang Dynasty's highly developed hierarchy consisted of a king, nobles, commoners, and slaves, who were known for their use of jade, bronze, horse-drawn chariots, ancestor worship, and highly organized armies.

The sovereignty of the Shang Dynasty lasted more than 500 years, until the Zhou Tribe rose from the Weishui River and replaced it.

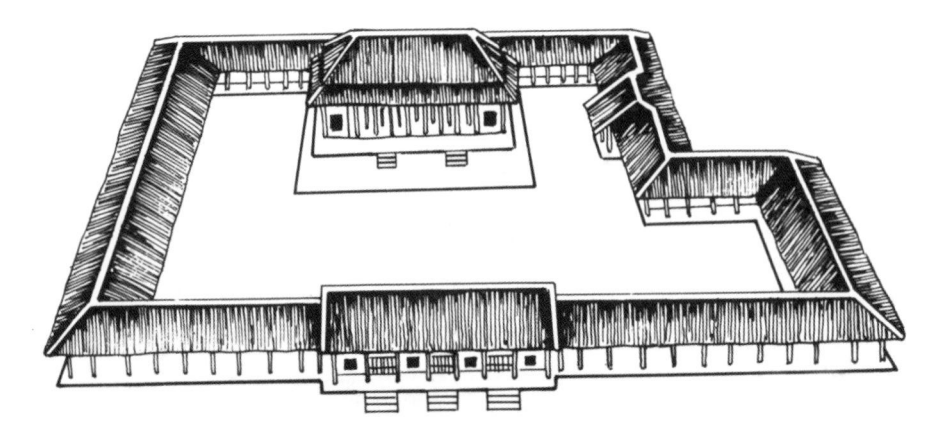

A drawing of restored palaces at the Erlitou Site.

Chapter 2 The Xia, Shang, and Western Zhou Dynasties 19

Jade image of a Shang Dynasty person, unearthed in the Fuhao Tomb of the Yin Ruins in Anyang, Henan.

Bronze *Ligui* of the Western Zhou Dynasty. Its 32-character inscription records the historical event of the punitive expedition to the Shang Dynasty by Emperor Wuwang of the Zhou Dynasty.

In 1046 BC, King Wu of the Zhou, together with more than 800 tribes, defeated the troops of King Zhou of the Shang Dynasty and established the Zhou Dynasty, called the Western Zhou, with its capital in Haojing (west of today's Xi'an, Shaanxi). During the Zhou Dynasty, the empire was unified, a middle class emerged, and iron replaced bronze for tools and weapons. And Confucius developed a code of ethics that has dominated Chinese thought and culture for over twenty-five centuries.

At the end of the nine centuries of Zhou rule, the Western Zhou Dynasty regime declined due to the rise of vassal lords. In 771 BC, the northwestern Quanrong ethnic group captured Haojing and killed Emperor Youwang, marking the end of the Western Zhou Dynasty.

Bronze Yu *Ding* (tripod cauldron) of the Western Zhou Dynasty. In the inner wall of the Ding, 291 engraved characters in 19 lines describe the conferment of an aristocratic title to Yu in the 23rd year of the reign of King Kang of the Zhou Dynasty, and the awarding of subjects and slaves to him. The Ding is a valuable artifact in the study of the Western Zhou feudal system.

Early States and Religious Society

Chinese civilization originated in the central plains, where an intensive agricultural economy prevailed and blood ties didn't collapse even during the centuries of civilization of society. The need for water control, for fighting external wars, and for handling other public affairs increasingly strengthened the blood-relation-based family organizations that connected the single, separated, natural agricultural economies. This further consolidated the rights and positions of clan leaders, who later became members of a new ruling class that integrated political power, religious authority, and financial and military power, and religious authority. In other words, clan-based organizations melted into state forms, shaping basic patterns for a patriarchal and feudal society.

People lived together in communities based on blood relations in the Xia and Shang dynasties. These clustering tribes were called *Fangguo* (Clan State). Leaders depended more on traditional clans and ties of kinship, and ruled on the basis of subordination among clans. The influence of this union of clan states didn't directly penetrate into neighboring kingdoms.

In the early Western Zhou Dynasty, the king established rituals as well as patriarchal and feudal systems to beef up the state's rule over neighboring regions, all of which resulted in intensified state administrative functions.

The patriarchal system was based on inheritance of land, property, and the position of blood relations. The King of Zhou, who called himself the "son of Heaven" and passed the throne of the Zhou Dynasty to the eldest son of his legal wife, was titled emperor of the state. The brothers of the eldest son would inherit part of the king's property and were honored as vassals or princes of the state, and they were supreme rulers within their own jurisdiction.

Based on the patriarchal principle, the system was designed to enroll the royal relatives in the feudal system, thereby cementing the rule of the Zhou Dynasty. The relatives were given "both citizens and land" and were supposed to manage local affairs, pay visits and tributes regularly, and offer services to fulfill their responsibility to safeguard the court. The feudal system, based on tenants of the same surname, broke the old kin-based state borders, and helped establish authority in some rich regions, key strategic areas, and military places. The resulting network, which reached from the central government down to the local areas, contributed to the country's stability and pushed the economic and cultural development of peripheral areas. In neighboring areas, a small number of relatives-in-law, ministers, and descendants of nobles were awarded "citizens and land" with a view to unifying other tribes and stabilizing political situations.

The Xia, Shang, and Western Zhou dynasties, which differentiated political positions based on kin relationships, were societies with stringent class hierarchies. As *The Commentary by Zuo on The Spring and Autumn Annals* goes, "There are ten social hierarchies, just as there are different days in life." The king ruled over ministers, who were superior to scholars, who were followed by servants at lower levels. Nobles with various privileges were often administrative officials at all levels, constituting the ruling class.

The imperial family and nobles owned many slaves. Prisoners or criminals, these slaves could be given away or sold. In addition to being used for hard labor, slaves were also killed as sacrifices to ancestors or buried alive with deceased nobles. More than 500 were offered as sacrifices in a single festival during the Shang Dynasty. However, strict patriarchal ties of kinship ensured that ordinary clansmen were not reduced to the status of "tools that could speak." The ordinary clansmen had their own families and means of production. As the main laborers of the agricultural and handicraft industry, they belonged to the civilian class and undertook services for the court and for nobles.

To conquer those outside and oppress those inside their kingdom, the Shang and Zhou dynasties maintained a powerful army. Jails and cruel criminal laws that involved execution, burying people alive, and cutting off the noses and feet of human beings were established as important means to maintain the reign of the nobles.

In the Xia, Shang, and Western Zhou dynasties, both nobles and civilians lived in social networks woven by clan or patriarchal ties. In addition to the establishment of the kin and region-integrated patriarchal clan and feudal systems, a series of ritual and musical systems used to regulate behavior were formulated to "differentiate and rank the nobles and the commoners" and to maintain the hierarchy and social order.

In the Western Zhou Dynasty, offering sacrifices to ancestors was equal in importance to wars, and was an important rite to safeguard the patriarchal clan system and enhance national integration. Guided by the idea of "destiny is conditional and favors those with virtues," the Zhou abandoned the Shang's blind belief in ghosts and gods and promoted the morality of respecting ancestors and the thought of "holding moral and caring people in high esteem." This helped to enlighten the people and to safeguard the hierarchical system and social order, showing a certain degree of rationalism.

By adopting a chain of innovative measures regarding government, Western Zhou Dynasty leaders cleverly combined kinship with the state regime, which helped stabilize the society, maintain the social order, and enhance national cohesion. In the meantime, breaking the old Xia and Shang dynasties' pattern of conflicts among independent clans also strengthened the king's

> ## FYI — FOR YOUR INFORMATION
>
> ### THE SQUARE-FIELDS SYSTEM
>
> The square-fields system adopted in the Shang and Zhou dynasties refers to farmland divided into square fields. Inside each square field, the crisscrossed ditches and paths resembled the Chinese character *Jing* (井). State-owned in name, the fields were actually owned by royal families and nobles. In exchange for certain tributes, civilians could use but not own them. No sales or transfers were allowed. Each field was divided into nine squares. The outer eight patches were private, the central one public. Village members were allowed to work in the "private fields" only after finishing work in the "public fields," for the nobles.

control over all parts of the state and pushed forward economic and cultural development in remote areas.

Brilliant Bronze Civilization

Both Shang and Western Zhou dynasties had more extensive territories than that of the Xia. Combined, they made up the largest country in the world. With rapid social and economic growth and the gradual maturity of the state form of rule, civilization during the Shang and Zhou made a great leap forward, mainly through the development of cities, the beginnings of a written language via inscriptions on bones and tortoise shells, and the creation of bronze from tin and copper.

The capital of the Shang covered an area of 30 million square meters, and boasted a population of 140,000 and a thriving commercial sector with "nine markets." The Western Zhou had 3 million citizens nationwide and saw even more development in urban cities, roads, accommodations, and postal services.

Ghost and god worship was popular in the Shang Dynasty. The nobles always cast lots in the event of sacrifices, war, fishing, hunting, and disease, among others. They engraved the results, known as "oracle inscriptions," on tortoise shells or bones. The ancient characters used are called *Jiaguwen*

Bronze *Jue* of the Xia Dynasty, unearthed at Erlitou, Yanshi County, Henan, is the earliest bronze vessel discovered in China to date.

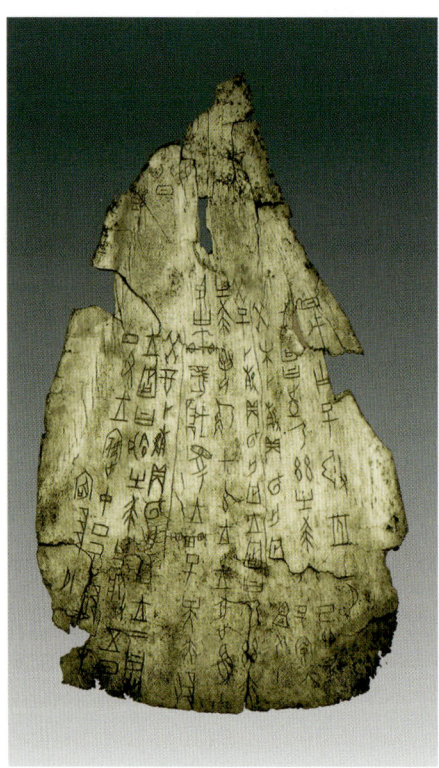

A piece of complete tortoise shell.

(inscriptions on bone or tortoise shell). Since the 19th century, more than 150,000 pieces of bone and shell with inscriptions have been unearthed, from places such as the Yin Ruins in Henan, indicating extensive use of *Jiaguwen* in the Shang Dynasty. Use of these ancient characters marked the start of China's recorded history.

Characters cast on bronze ware from the Western Zhou Dynasty are called *Jinwen* (inscriptions on bronze). *Jiaguwen* and *Jinwen* incorporated six kinds of character-shaping principles, including pictography, pictophonetic compounds, ideographs, logical aggregates, associative transformation, and borrowing, paving the way for the development of Chinese characters. A total of 4,500 *Jiaguwen* characters have been found so

Oracle inscription on ox bones saying "farming together" documents the Shang Dynasty Monarch's order to his subjects to till lands jointly.

far. While the number of *Jinwen* characters increased greatly, so did passage lengths, including one long inscription with nearly 500 characters. *Jiaguwen* and *Jinwen* are the forerunners of the Chinese characters used today. Extensive use of characters indicates that social development had reached a higher stage. The use of a writing system goes beyond time and space, as it records the thoughts, language, and experiences of human beings and documents intricate natural and social phenomena. This enabled communication and tradition and greatly drove cultural development forward.

The development of the bronze casting industry during the Shang and Zhou dynasties greatly increased what people could produce and hence their quality of life. About 10,000 pieces of bronze ware cast in the Shang Dynasty have so far been unearthed.

More than 5,000 pieces came from the tombs of the Guo Kingdom of the Western Zhou Dynasty. The tombs' bronze pieces were primarily weapons, like

Bronze *Zhao You* of the Western Zhou Dynasty. Inside is a forty-four-character inscription that describes the Monarch of Zhou's awarding 50 square *li* (12.4 square kilometers) in the Bi area to Zhao, important evidence for the study of the square-fields system.

Bronze bell chimes of the Western Zhou Dynasty. Chimes were the main ritual instruments played at sacrifices, banquets, and other events of nobles.

daggers, spears, battle-axes, and arrowheads, and tools like knives and axes, as well as a few fittings for carriages and farm tools.

Bronze mining, smelting, and casting techniques matured in the Shang Dynasty. The site of an ancient copper mine from the Western Zhou, located in Tonglü Mountain, Daye, Hubei, covers an area of about 2 square kilometers at a depth of 60 meters. Silos, inclined alleys, and flat valleys, were adopted for excavation. Drainage systems were built, and ventilation problems inside the mine were resolved as well. Residue from the ancient mine contains a copper content of only 0.7 percent. The craftsmen of the Shang Dynasty could accurately calculate the proper proportions of copper and tin, and made bronze of different hardness.

Shang and Zhou bronze ware was famous not only for their great number and diverse categories, but also for their spectacular shapes and superb craftsmanship. The Simuwu Ding, unearthed in the Yin Ruins, is grand in size and exquisite in pattern. The largest extant bronze piece in the world, it is 133 centimeters high and weighs more than 800 kilograms. The majestic bronze Ding is a symbol of the brilliant civilization of the Shang and Zhou dynasties.

The Simuwu Bronze Ding of the Shang Dynasty, unearthed in Wuguan Village, Anyang, Henan, is the heaviest bronze piece discovered in China to date.

Ancient Egypt, ancient Babylon, and the Harappan culture in the Indus River Valley, which coexisted with China's Xia and Shang dynasties, successively declined after creating splendid civilizations. However, the rise and fall of the Xia, Shang, and Zhou dynasties accumulated the successive genes of the Chinese culture in the form of bronze production technology, and in the use of written language as a way to communicate cultural values forward. The gradually maturing political system, social structure, and rituals of the early states had a profound influence on later generations.

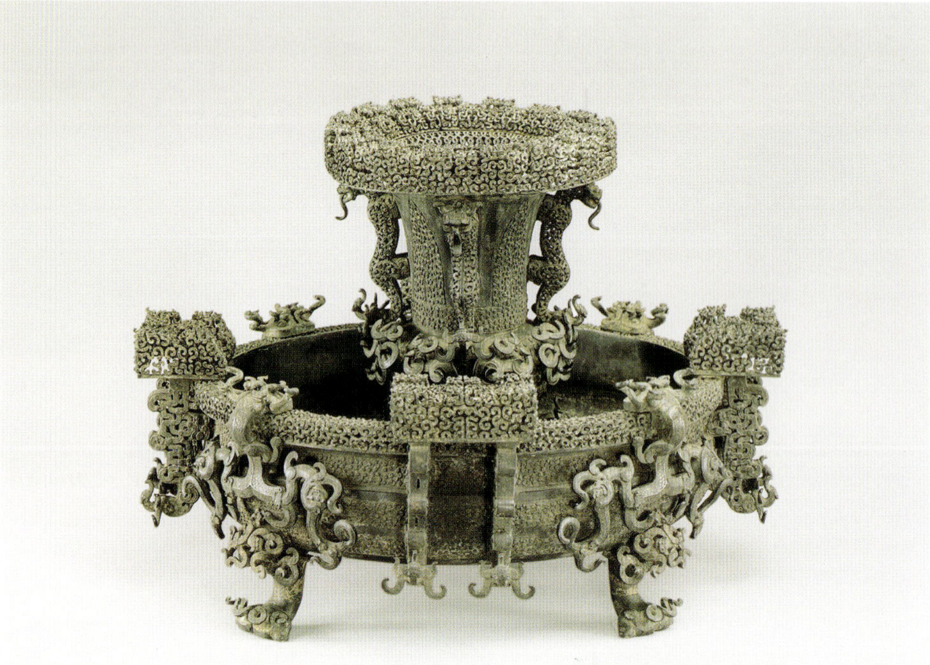

Chapter 3

The Spring and Autumn and Warring States Periods: States Contend for Power, Control, and Social Reform

The Five Powers in the Spring and Autumn Period and the Seven States in the Warring States Period

In 770 BC, the second year after the Western Zhou Dynasty ended, King Ping of the Zhou Dynasty relocated the capital to Luoyi (today's Luoyang, Henan), known as the Eastern Zhou in history. The Spring and Autumn Period (770–477 BC) was named after the State of Lu's chronicle *The Spring and Autumn Annals,* and the Warring States Period (477–221 BC) after the conflicts among states for the throne.

During this 550-year period, the territory governed by the court declined, shrinking to a radius of 600 *li* (300 kilometers). Vassals stopped paying visits and tributes, and the king, therefore, had to "announce a state of hunger" and "beg for money and chariots." He thus became highly dependent on the vassals. King Huan of the Zhou Dynasty, shot by troops of the Zheng, lost his dignity as a king. Tenants waged hundreds of wars against each other.

Duke Huan of Qi took power in the Spring and Autumn Period. He named Guan Zhong as the prime minister, who later launched large-scale reforms. Economically, Guan Zhong encouraged trade and the reclaiming of barren land. Militarily, he organized strong armies. Politically, he promoted the slogan of "respecting the king and dispelling aliens," joining hands with all the states

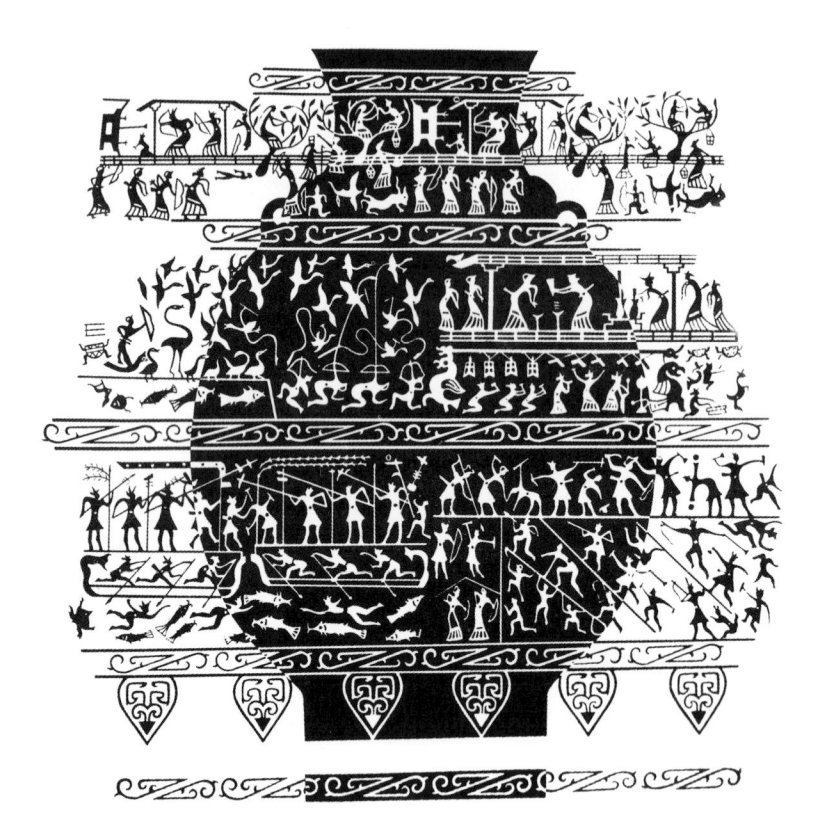

Land and Water Battle Scenes inscribed on a bronze kettle from the Warring States Period, unearthed in Chengdu, Sichuan.

in the central plains and working to safeguard Chinese culture. In 651 BC, the State of Qi initiated a meeting of all the vassals in Kuiqiu, which the king of the Zhou Dynasty sent a representative to attend. That established the position of Duke Huan of Qi in the central plains.

The states of Jin and Chu rose successively after the State of Qi. After decades of exile, Duke Wen of Jin returned to his home state, taking the throne and making vigorous efforts to rejuvenate his country. Defeating the troops of Chu in the Battle of Chengpu in 632 BC, he organized a meeting of all vassals where his leadership position was established. The State of Chu in the South thrived once again after Duke Zhuang took office. In 606 BC, the troops of Chu threatened Luoyi, capital of the Zhou Dynasty, and Chu brazenly asked about the size and weight of the *Ding* of Zhou, exposing his ambition to replace the king. Before long his troops marched northward once again, defeating the troops of Jin at Bi and ensuring the domination of Duke Zhuang of Chu.

A portrait brick of Duke Huan of Qi and his minister Guan Zhong.

In the late Spring and Autumn Period, the states of Wu and Yue in the South rose to power in succession. The State of Wu in the lower reaches of the Yangtze River captured the capital of the State of Chu in 506 BC. It also later swallowed the State of Yue in the Qiantang River basin, defeated the troops of Qi in the North, and met all the vassals at Huangchi, Henan. King Goujian of Yue, after being defeated and captured, endured much humiliation and hardship for twenty years. But he finally conquered Gusu, the capital of Wu, by dispatching troops after King Fuchai of Wu had squandered the national wealth. Years later, he further annexed the State of Wu and marched into the central plains, becoming the last leader in the Spring and Autumn Period.

In the early Warring States Period, the patriarchal and feudal system was destroyed and the king's privileges were transferred to lower levels. Some ministers and senior officials, who grew to be important players through implementing reforms, gradually carved up and replaced the privileges and positions of former vassals, paving their way into positions of power. In 403 BC, the

The sword of Gou Jian, King of Yue.

states of Han, Zhao, and Wei divided the State of Jin, and Tianshi, a senior official of Qi, replaced Jiangshi to become the vassal. The wars among vassals got more frequent, resulting in a pattern where seven powers, known as the states of Han, Zhao, Wei, Qi, Chu, Yan, and Qin, coexisted and fought against each other to seek power and control. Following the dominance of Dukes Wen of Wei in the central plains, the war between Qi and Wei, and the confrontation between Qin and Qi, the State of Qin grew strong through Shang Yang's reforms. Qin defeated the troops of Zhao at Changping in 260 BC, which led to the rise of Qin and the chaotic situation of "vertical alliance and horizontal collaboration."

Chapter 3 The Spring and Autumn and Warring States Periods

Bronze mirror, unearthed in Yunmeng, Hubei, with patterns of warriors of the Qin State during the Warring States Period fighting beasts, showing the belligerent character of the people of Qin after Shang Yang's reform.

The wars of the Spring and Autumn and Warring States period brought serious disasters to the people and broke the old social order, paving the way for a new system. The five powers of the Spring and Autumn Period—namely Qi, Jin, Chu, Wu, and Yue (or Qi, Song, Jin, Qin, and Chu)—and the seven states of the Warring States—namely Qi, Chu, Yan, Qin, Han, Zhao, and Wei—all worked for reform and rose toward a new reunification.

FYI — FOR YOUR INFORMATION

VERTICAL ALLIANCE AND HORIZONTAL COLLABORATION

Seven powers strove to seek hegemony in the Warring States Period. Besides using military force, each state also resorted to political and diplomatic means. The six eastern states joined hands to form a south-north vertical alliance to confront the State of Qin, called the "vertical alliance." Meanwhile, the State of Qin, located in the west, took advantage of the conflicts among the eastern states, and tactically went into collaboration with part of the six states and finally attacked all of them one by one, called a "horizontal collaboration." The eastern states sometimes followed the State of Qin and sometimes followed the State of Chu for the sake of their own interests. Some advisors, like Su Qin and Zhang Yi, traveled around the states, persuading vassals to adopt a vertical alliance or a horizontal collaboration and were called "Men of Alliance and Collaboration."

Social Reforms Triggered by the Use of Iron Tools and the Use of Oxen to Plow

The Spring and Autumn Period witnessed profound reforms and changes in ancient Chinese society. Improvement in tools and techniques were the underlying cause of large-scale social reforms.

The Iron Age starts from the Spring and Autumn Period. Hard, sharp, iron tools replaced wood and stone instruments in agricultural production. In the Warring States Period, iron plows drawn by two oxen were used, promoting ease of cultivation. Large-scale compulsory collective cultivation was the norm. Historical records of "being slow for collective cultivation while working quickly for private land" reflect the profound reforms that resulted from the ability of an individual with oxen to plow land. Thanks to the improved efficiency, a great deal of barren land was reclaimed. Products reaped from the extra private land were no longer presented to the kings. Owners of these private lands leased it to peasants and collected rent, which greatly aroused the production enthusiasm of individual peasants. Inefficient, backward, collective cultivation of "public fields" was strongly opposed, leading to stretches of weedy, uncultivated land. The vassals, therefore, had to lease the "public fields" to peasants for cultivation, marking the collapse of the square-fields system. A landowner economy, based on land privatization and individual cultivation, rapidly expanded.

The surge in private property ownership and private cultivation broke the old system of the patriarchal nobles' hereditary occupation of fiefs and their military and political power, abolished their hereditary privileges in position and salary, and initiated reforms aimed at developing a private property economy, enriching the country and forging a mighty army.

Guan Zhong of the State of Qi in the Spring and Autumn Period initiated a policy of "collecting tributes and taxes according to the size and quality of land." The State of Lu implemented a policy of "initial tax on land per-mu," which provided that taxes be levied based on actual land size regardless of ownership. These tax reforms, in nature, confirmed the validity of privately owned land in the form of state laws. Later on, the State of Qin launched a policy

An iron sword with gold nose and head, unearthed in Houchuan, Shanxian, Henan, Spring and Autumn Period.

Chapter 3   The Spring and Autumn and Warring States Periods

of "destroying square fields and allowing land sales," which further legalized and popularized privately owned land and paved the way for the state's ruling over landowners.

Li Kui, appointed by Duke Wen of the State of Wei in the Warring States Period, worked out *The Book of Law* to beef up rules regarding private property. Duke Dao of the State of Chu appointed Wu Qi to reform the old hereditary and official administration systems, thereby consolidating the centralized monarchy. The reform confronted fierce resistance, as it was damaging to the interests of the old nobles. For instance, after Duke Dao of the State of Chu passed away, the conservative side killed Wu Qi, who had been hiding at the side of the King's body for shelter. However, after many setbacks, reforms took place in Qi, Jin, Zheng, Wu, Yue, Wei, Chu, Qin, Han, Zhao, Yan, and other vassal states, including Shang Yang's Political Reform in the State of Qin, in the middle Warring States Period.

In 356 BC, Duke Xiao of the State of Qin appointed Shang Yang to launch political reform, which included rewarding cultivation and feats in battle, abolishing the square-fields system and field boundaries, and establishing a county system. The new law abolished the hereditary position and salary system and set up twenty ranks for political and economic privileges to be awarded based solely on performance. The reform subverted the nobles' privileges and improved the morale and battle-effectiveness of the army. It also ruled that those who achieved a high output of grain and cloth would be exempt from duty service and taxes, thereby inspiring production activity and improving state power. "Abolishing the square-fields system and the field boundaries" refers to opening the boundaries of the square fields occupied by the nobles and admitting the legality of private land. The new law also divided the State of Qin into 31 (or 41) counties to replace the old system. The county magistrates and assistants were appointed and

Mold for simultaneous casting of two iron sickles of the Warring States Period, unearthed in Gudonggou, Xinglong County, Hebei.

A *Zun* tray unearthed from Marquis Yi of Zeng's Tomb in Suixian County, Hubei, showcases the remarkable casting process and sophisticated bronze technology of the Warring States Period.

dismissed by the duke, and no hiring of kin was allowed. The State of Qin also compiled household registrations and implemented penalties that implicated those related to the one charged or found guilty. Normally, five or ten families formed a unit to supervise one another. In addition, Shang Yang formulated Qin rules and uniform standards of weight and measurement, making great contributions to unification.

Shang Yang carried out two stages of reform in the State of Qin over a period of twenty years, gradually making Qin powerful and rich. Shang Yang executed laws rigidly. He cut off the nose and tattooed the face of the Prince's tutor and that of anyone who suborned the Prince to block reform. When the Prince came into power, Shang Yang was executed by being fastened to five chariots and pulled apart. But the laws continued and the new policies prevailed. The rapid rise of Qin in the remote western areas in the later Warring States period was largely attributed to Shang Yang's new policy. A century after the death of Shang Yang, Duke Yingzheng of Qin

The Square Bronze Sheng made by Shang Yang is a standard bronze measuring instrument that unified the metrology of the Qin State.

took advantage of the influence of Shang Yang's reform to help accelerate the pace of national unification.

Qin paid great attention to agriculture, laying a solid economic foundation for unification. The Dujiangyan Irrigation Project built by Qin's Shu County Major Li Bing continues to irrigate thousands of *mu*[1] of land, making the Chengdu Plain a fertile place, free of starvation caused by flood and drought. The Zhengguo Channel, constructed in the Weihe River Plain under the leadership of Zheng Guo, irrigated 2.8 million *mu* of farmland, creating another enormous granary in the central Shanxi Plain.

The policy of honoring military exploits forged a brave army. The tri-ridge arrows unearthed from the Qin's terracotta warriors and horses pit were sharp enough to penetrate armor. The six states' military force could not do anything but escape in the face of the Qin army, whose overwhelming power was described as "a heavy weight on bird's eggs."

Enterprising policies and leaders being open enough to absorb the merits of other states were important factors for Qin's unification. In 238 BC, shortly after Duke Yingzheng of Qin came into power, the state of Han sent Zheng Guo to persuade Yingzheng to dig a channel in the Jinghe basin to divert water for irrigation, a request intended to exhaust the national strength of Qin and hinder its pace of marching eastward. But the plot failed before the channel was built and Zheng Guo was arrested. Zheng argued that building the channel could do nothing but offer a few years more for the State of Han, even though it consumed a great deal of fiscal revenue. But for the State of Qin, the great project would benefit later generations. Hearing this, Yingzheng changed his mind and let Zheng continue its construction.

---

[1] A Chinese unit of area. 1 *mu* equals 666.6 square meters.

Dujiangyan Irrigation System, constructed under the leadership of Li Bing and his son, still plays a role in flood control and irrigation today.

Some patriarchal ministers of Qin argued that ministers of foreign origin should be dismissed since they came to Qin for persuasion and estrangement. Li Si, a minister from Chu, submitted "Remonstrance on Dispelling Ministers of Foreign Origin" to refute them with the instances that the dukes of Qin used ministers of foreign origin to build Qin.

Yingzheng then became aware of the importance of foreign ministers and cancelled the order for dispelling ministers and called Li Si back. He and other foreign ministers played an active role in helping Yingzheng unify the other six states into one country.

From 230 BC to 221 BC, Yingzheng directed his army to conquer six states and established the first centralized empire in Chinese history.

Instances of vassals contending for hegemony and progress in social reform were interwoven into the period. Collapsed ritualism and musical systems and social turmoil offered an open space for reform in states. Reform was the only way to make the country and army powerful enough to win the competition. Warfare for merging and seizing power was endowed with the added significance of expanding reform and new policies.

Cultural Awakening and Contention of a Hundred Schools of Thought

In the late Spring and Autumn Period and the Warring States Period, iron tools and ox-plow farming enhanced productivity, boosted commerce and town prosperity, and seriously impacted the traditional ritual order. In the reform fever of various states, a batch of scholars broke the parochial clan network and moved freely. They maneuvered among various political groups and gave lectures here and there, greatly enlarging their field of vision and promoting cultural awakening.

In the Spring and Autumn Period, the pattern of "cultural learning exclusive to officials and nobles" was broken, and the scholars' "private schools" for spreading culture gradually prevailed. For instance, Confucius of the State of Lu vigorously promoted the thought of "education for all." He had more than 3,000 disciples, including 72 famous ones, some of humble birth. Widespread education paved the way for a booming culture in this period of transformation.

An intensive yeoman economy showed greater advantage over simple and extensive farming, which further aroused the enthusiasm of the producers. Furthermore, the highly-developed handicraft and commercial sectors and the reforms in all states aimed at building a more prosperous society helped achieve great scientific and technological progress in the Spring and Autumn and Warring States periods. Bronze casting techniques matured, resulting in a vast number of superb bronze artworks. Raw iron could be smelted as early as the Spring and Autumn Period, and cast iron techniques were invented in the Warring States Period, 2,000 years earlier than those in the West. The Spring and Autumn Period saw the production of the world's earliest cementite steel. The Warring States Period witnessed the accomplishment of the Dujiangyan Irrigation System, built by the masses and led by Li Bing and his son. The irrigation system, consisting of the fish-mouth water diversion dike, bottleneck and flying, and weir, was able to prevent and drain floods, as well as irrigate and carry boats. It helped the Chengdu Plain develop into a land of abundance, and today irrigates tens of millions of *mu* of land.

The *Shi Star Catalog,* the world's first star catalog, recorded the positions of more than 120 stars, and recorded the world's earliest observations of comets in 613 BC. Arithmetically, the 9x9 Formula for Multiplication and the Method of Count Calculating were invented. The *Mohist Canon,* written in the Warring States Period, includes the Lever Principle and the Theory of Buoyancy, as well as knowledge about acoustics and optics—outstanding achievements in ancient China. Medically, Bian Que, a famous doctor in the Warring States Period, established the theory of four diagnostic procedures, namely inspection, auscultation (listening to the sounds of internal organs) and olfaction (attention to odors), inquiry, and pulse-taking and palpation. Chinese doctors have used these Oriental medicine procedures for 2,000 years. Bian Que was thus reputed as the "ancestor of Chinese pulse-taking science."

Great scientific advances sped up the awakening of rationalism and cultural spirit. The Spring and Autumn Period saw the emergence of China's first poetry collection, *The Book of Odes,* a compilation of 305 odes written during the 500 years from the early Western Zhou to the middle Spring and Autumn Period. The book has three parts, namely *Feng, Ya,* and *Song.* The *Feng* section (also named Guofeng) is of the highest quality. Its folk songs include satires on the ruling class, praises for popular protest, and wishes for beautiful love. In simple and rich language, *The Book of Odes* contains four-character lines and many refrains, marking the birth of Chinese poetry. The inclination toward realism and use of rhetorical devices such as *Fu* (straightforward narrative), *Bi* (explicit comparisons), and *Xing* (implied comparisons) had a far-reaching influence on poets of later generations.

Chapter 3 The Spring and Autumn and Warring States Periods

Portrait of Qu Yuan.

In the subsequent Warring States Period, Chu odes, a new form of poetry based on folk songs in the state of Chu in the south, emerged and became popular, because its free-style sentences were more suitable for expressing complicated feelings.

Written by Qu Yuan, *The Lament,* a collection of famous works in Chu odes form, expressed his political aspirations and patriotic feelings. The poems feature the repeated use of symbols and metaphors, and combine myth, legend, historical figures, and natural scenes with magnificent words, distinctive imagination, strong feelings, and profound concepts.

The *Book of Odes,* with *Guofeng* as its representative, and the Chu odes, with *The Lament* as their representative, are collectively referred to as *Feng Sao,* which reflects the emergence of an early cultural spirit and started the realistic and romantic styles, respectively, of ancient Chinese poetry.

Portrait of Confucius.

Two great thinkers with far-reaching influence on Chinese history emerged in the Spring and Autumn Period—Confucius and Lao Tze.

Confucius, named Qiu and style-named Zhongni, was a thinker of the State of Lu. His thoughts were mainly recorded in *The Analects of Confucius,* a book compiled by his disciples. The essence of Confucianism is *Ren* (benevolence) and *Li* (ritual norms). He advocated the idea that "the benevolent loves his fellow people," and requested the rulers experience and observe the situation of the people. He was against tyranny and arbitrary punishment. He advocated the codes of loyalty and tolerance, and called for "not doing to others what you don't want to be done to you" (do unto others as you would have them do unto you) and understanding others as a way to harmonize personal relationships and stabilize the social order.

Confucius also valued "ruling by morality" and "ruling with the ritual norms." He saw that one could maintain the political and educational system of the country by encouraging self restraint, restoring rituals, and practicing moral behavior. He attempted to correct the chaotic social class order in accordance with the ritual system of the Zhou Dynasty and make it perfectly justifiable, reflecting his conservative political ideology. However, Confucius was not against improving and reforming obsolete ritual customs and political orders on the basis of maintaining an outdated social class system.

Chapter 3 The Spring and Autumn and Warring States Periods

Mencius and Xun Zi in the Warring States Period inherited and developed Confucius' theory and made the political ideals and moral norms of Confucianism the mainstream of traditional thought in China for more than two millennia.

Lao Tze, surnamed Li, named Er, and style-named Dan, was a thinker of the State of Chu. Erudite and knowledgeable, he was once the historical official in the royal court of the Eastern Zhou, responsible for managing collections. Confucius once asked Lao Tze about "ritual norms."

The *Tao Te Ching,* a book compiled by the followers of Taoism in the Warring States Period, records the thought of Lao Tze and is replete with the philosophy and wisdom typical of the oriental world. Lao Tze denied the absolute authority of destiny, advocated following natural laws, and ruling without intervention. "Ruling without intervention" means not intervening arbitrarily. Lao Tze warned the rulers not to oppress the common people too much.

However, his ideal that "though the noises made by the chickens and dogs can be heard, the people do not contact each other until death" and his concept of "making the people ignorant and without desire" led to some negative effects. His philosophy is rich in dialectic thinking. Lao Tze pointed out that everything has two contradictory

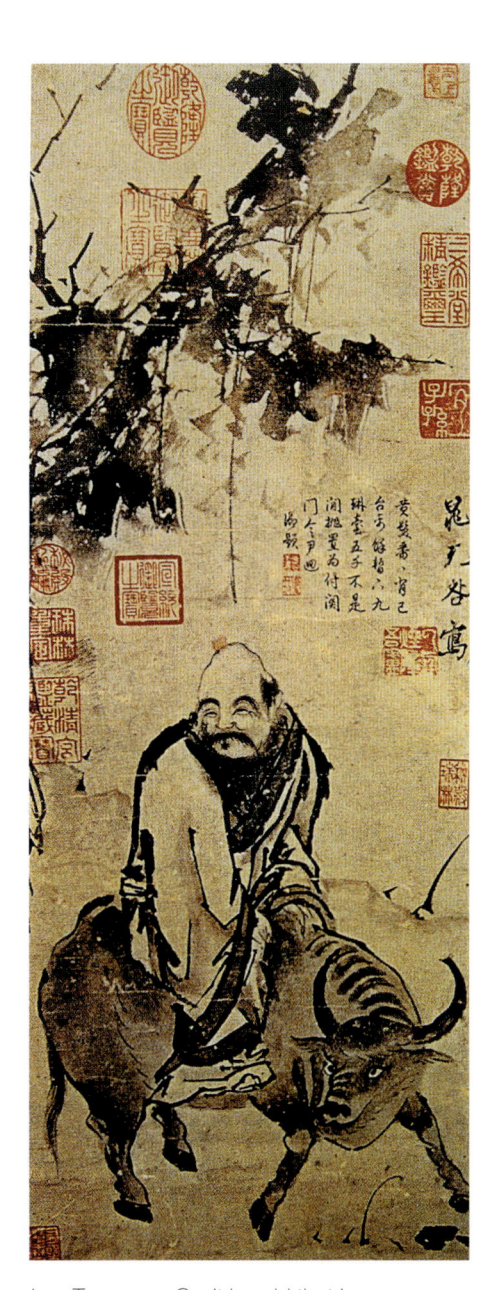

Lao Tze on an Ox. It is said that Lao Tze, seeing that the Zhou Dynasty was declining, rode an ox out of the Hangu Pass and vanished from the earthly life.

Portrait of Mencius.

sides, for example—high and low, front and rear, existence and void, difficult and easy, life and death, noble and humble—and everything could shift to the opposite. Lao Tze has been regarded by later generations as the founder of Taoism. His thought has had and continues to have a great influence on Chinese culture, including philosophy and ethics, as well as the mode of thinking, morality, and personality of the Chinese people.

The increasingly intense competition among all vassal states for power and control in the Warring States Period led to a more urgent need for talented people. The profound social reforms offered those scholars with an expanded consciousness a broad stage for independent thinking and creative exploration.

Duke Xuan of Qi had hotels built near Jimen, Linzi, capital of Qi to accommodate literary talents and persuasive talkers, and awarded scholars such as Zou Yan, Tian Pian, and Shen Dao mansions and official titles to encourage them to write books and establish theories. The scholars' hotels at Jimen then grew into a center for communication among various academic schools. Representatives from different classes and schools offered different opinions on different issues and held discussions with one another, resulting in "contention of a hundred schools of thought."

Among the active schools of thought were Confucianism, the Mohist School, Taoism, Legalism, the Yin-Yang School, the School of Names, the Military School, and the School of Eclectics.

Mencius and Xun Zi were the representatives of Confucianism in the Warring States Period. Mencius further developed Confucius' "benevolence" into a systematic political doctrine, proposing the concept that "The people are the most important element in a state; next are the gods of land and grain; least is the ruler himself." He also stressed that "righteousness comes first and then the benefit" and "giving one's life for righteousness" is commendable. He is particularly known for his aphorism that one should "never be corrupted by wealth or title, never depart from your principles when in poverty and hardship, and surrender never to power and force." Xun Zi said that ruling a state should be based on ritual norms and supplemented by laws. He also held the opinion that "nature has its laws" and they won't be changed by human will, but humans should give play to their abilities to "make use of the objective laws" and thus benefit themselves.

The founder of Mohist School was Mo Tzu, a man of humble birth in the State of Lu. Once a craftsman, he later became a senior official of the State of Song. Mo Tzu advocated "universal love," going far beyond the concept of "benevolence" based on different classes proposed by Confucius. He considered all people to be equal, whether nobles or commoners. He also upheld "respecting the wise," employing talented people regardless of class, and proposed "respecting the working people," stressing the position of labor in the society. Mo Tzu opposed extravagance and waste, and advocated "thrift in daily life and funerals."

The book *Mo Tzu* also greatly contributes to natural science and logical science. The Mohist School reflects the interests of the working class, especially those of craftsmen.

Zhuang Tzu inherited and developed the thoughts of Lao Tze and was the representative of Taoism in the Warring States Period. Named Zhou and born in the State of Song, he despised wealth and fame, and hated the unfair social phenomena of "stealing ideas from one person is plagiarism, and stealing ideas from many is research." He once refused the request of the Duke of Chu to be a senior official, and instead earned a living by making straw sandals and wrote books for recreation. Zhuang Tzu upheld the idea that "natural law" has its own roots and everything is the same in nature. On this basis, he put forward a playful living attitude of pondering over nothing, and worrying about nothing. He pointed out that "dimensions are limitless, and time is endless." He recognized the infinity of time and space and believed that humans need only obey the natural laws. Politically, Zhuang Tzu upheld the thought of ruling without intervention.

Han Fei, a philosopher of the late Warring States Period, was an integrator of Legalism. In his philosophy, the ruler firmly controls the state with the help of three concepts—his position of power (*Shi*), certain techniques (*Shu*), and laws (*Fa*)—to set up a monarchic despotism. He believed laws were the basis of handling state affairs, techniques were the tools for the emperor to control the ministers, and power was the regime and influence of the emperor. He

Portrait of Zhuang Tzu.

advocated "ruling a state according to law" and that "laws don't protect powerful persons," which was of positive significance for attacking the privileges of former nobles and maintaining the emerging centralized system of private property ownership.

Han Fei believed that society keeps developing and changing, and that history will never repeat itself. He was against the historical concept of Confucians, "confirming the ancient practice and denying today's practice," and advocated reform. In his opinion, ruling the people with the politics of ancient kings was as ridiculous as standing by a tree stump waiting for a hare to dash itself against it. Han Fei's philosophy met the requirements of establishing a centralized regime and was embraced by Yingzheng, which made Han's philosophy the guiding concept of ruling the country.

In the thousand years since the Western Han Dynasty, Han Fei's thought and Confucianism supported each other and became the theoretical

Portrait of Han Fei.

foundation of the ruling thought of ancient China. The spirit of reform became the theoretical weapon for progressive thinkers and politicians in the following generations.

Leaders of the Yin-Yang school of thought that emerged in the late Warring States Period popularized the Theory of Five Elements, that is, "Metal, Wood, Water, Fire, and Earth." Social evolution, according to the Yin-Yang School, mirrors the cyclic changes of the five elements, the "natural laws" that control everything. Representatives of this school of thought include Zou Yan of the State of Qi, who had a great influence on the social ideology in the Qin and Han dynasties.

The School of Names, represented by Hui Shi and Gongsun Long, analyzed and "rectified" the situation where names (words) were mixed up with objects in times of social reform. Followers viewed the similarity-difference relations from a philosophical perspective, and pointed out the distinctions between feelings and objective facts, as well as existence and attributes. This helped develop logic in China.

The founder of the Military School was Sun Wu, a stragetist in the Spring and Autumn Period. His *Art of War* reveals many tactics of deploying troops as well as military laws, such as exercising systematic and overall control. His complete system of military theories is considered a classic book of military science that can ensure "fighting a hundred battles with no danger of defeat" and enjoys a truly high reputation worldwide.

The representative of the Military School in the Warring States Period was Sun Bin, a descendant of Sun Wu. As the military advisor of Qi, Sun Bin once directed the classic battle known as "saving the Zhao by besieging the capital of the Wei." Inheriting the thoughts of Sun Wu, he stressed commanding the rules of war and creating favorable situations for oneself, and he emphasized the role of the individual. His military thoughts were compiled into the book *Sun Bin's Art of War,* which exists in bamboo-slip versions from the Han Dynasty.

The School of Eclectics, shaped in the late Warring States Period, was a combination of the above. Lu's *Spring and Autumn Annals* is its most famous representative work. Focusing on the idea of "acting according to the ways of nature," the book integrates many schools of thought on the topic of state-governing politics. The Eclectics held that kings should respect teachers and advocate education, put public interests in front of their own, employ talented people, and rule with no arbitrary intervention. Kings should also follow the will of the people and unify the country with righteous armies.

The argument among the pre-Qin schools and their mutual influence greatly helped promote intellectual and cultural progress. The creative concepts and theories established in all these works cover many fields, including politics, economy, military science, laws, education, philosophy, history, literature, art, and natural science, jointly constituting the original classics that guide Chinese ideology today and the fundamental spirit of traditional Chinese culture.

Around the 5th century BC, both Eastern and Western civilization reached a high level of development. They jointly created a spectacle that marked the start of a brand new era in human history. The city-state democratic politics of ancient Greece, established on the basis of a slavery economy, gave rise to such great thinkers as Socrates, Plato, and Aristotle. Meanwhile the profound yeoman reforms and social transformation in China's Spring and Autumn and Warring States periods created an ideal environment for the rise of many cultural masters, like Confucius and Lao Tze. The philosophers of both east and west jointly built numerous lofty monuments for human civilization.

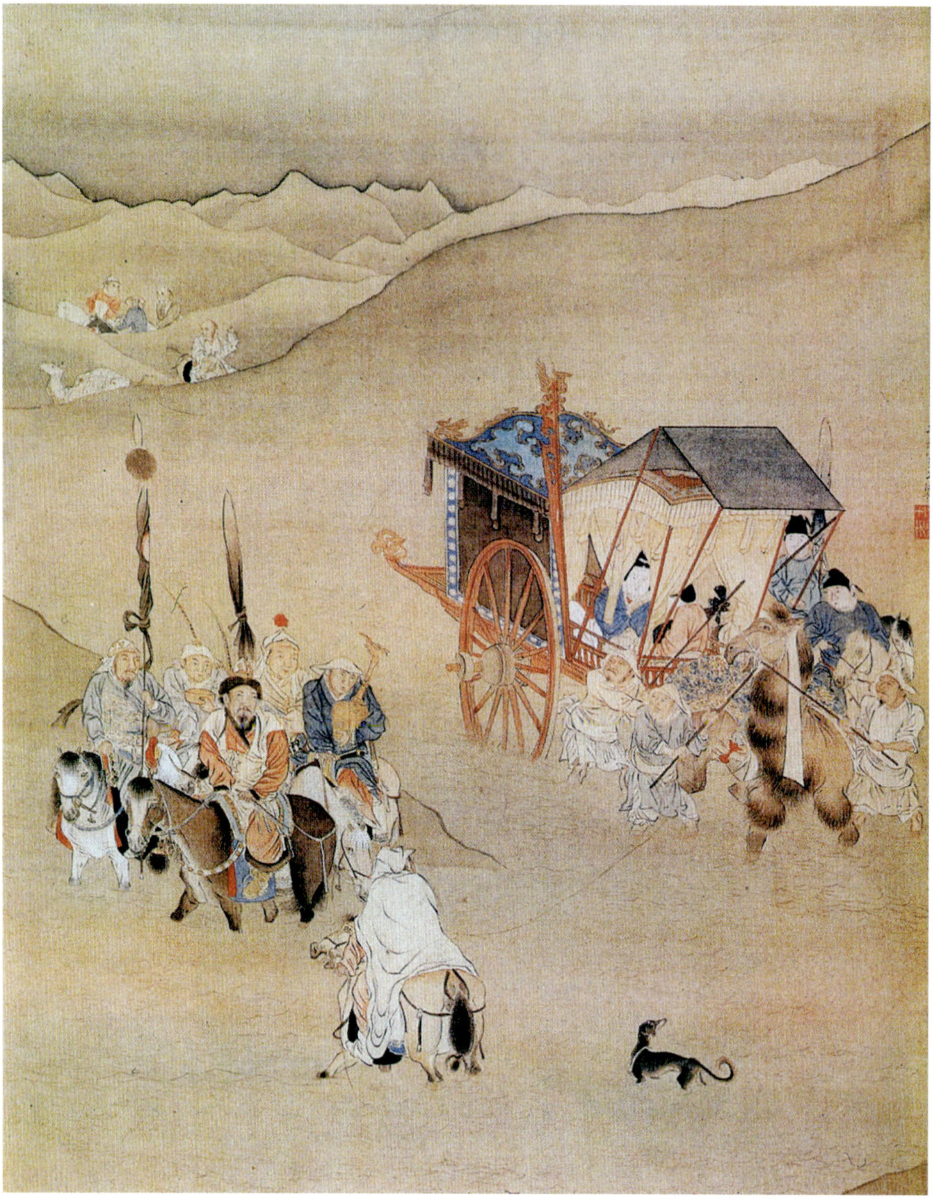

Chapter 4

The Qin and Han Dynasties: Establishment and Development of a Great Unified Country

Qin Dynasty Lays the Foundation for the Great Unification

The Qin and Han dynasties, from 221 BC to 220 AD, were the first unified multiethnic centralized states in Chinese history, laying the foundation for a united empire.

In 221 BC, Qin continued expansion outward after annexing the six states. It suppressed the Baiyue people on the southeastern coast and in southern China and the ethnic groups in southwestern areas and established administrative organs there for unified management. Qin's troops also attacked the Huns in the north, regained the Great Bend of the Yellow River for its people to migrate to and cultivate, and constructed the Great Wall to consolidate its northern defense. Finally, Qin established an unprecedented vast empire with a population of 20 million multiethnic people.

Yingzheng, after unifying the six states, called himself "Shihuangdi" (the first emperor) because "his virtues were equal to the Three August Ones (Fu Xi, Nu Wa, and Shen Nong) and his merits were greater than those of the Five Emperors (Huangdi, Zhuan Xu, Di Ku, Yao, and Shun)." After establishing his supreme power, he carried on the social reforms that started during the Spring and Autumn and the Warring States periods and implemented a series of measures to intensify centralized sovereignty.

With respect to the political system, Emperor Shihuang believed that the feudal system was the source of the ceaseless wars of the Spring and Autumn

Portrait of Emperor Shihuang of the Qin Dynasty.

Period and thought "it's time to set up armies because peace has returned and the country is unified." He accepted the suggestion of Li Si to award his sons and the officials who performed deeds of great merit in ways other than giving them an estate, and further established a complete set of bureaucratic administration systems at both central and local levels.

The emperor controlled the country's military power, and his descendants inherited the throne from generation to generation. At the central level were three chief ministers and nine departments. The "three chief ministers" referred to the prime minister, military minister, and supervision minister. The prime minister assisted the emperor in handling political affairs and led all other officials. The military minister assisted the emperor in military affairs, and the supervision minister was responsible for supervision and law enforcement as well as literature management. The three ministers were not subject to one another and all obeyed the emperor's orders.

The nine departments included the administrative organizations at the central level and those in charge of royal affairs. The system established imperial power as supreme, and the prime minister as the leading official. All officials were responsible for their own business. This has laid a foundation for the organizational pattern of Chinese central government.

The emperor established two levels of administrative organizations nationwide, namely prefectures and counties, and shaped their local bureaucratic administrative systems. The prefecture, the higher-level administrative organ of the central government, directly governed the local. The supreme executive of the prefecture was named the prefecture governor (*Junshou*). The *Juncheng* (prefecture governor's assistant) helped the prefecture governor handle administrative affairs, criminal punishment, and prison affairs, while the *Junwei* (prefecture governor's assistant officer) was in charge of military affairs and public security.

County governments were set up under the prefecture. The responsibilities of the county executive, county executive's assistant, and county executive's assistant officer were similar to those of the officials at the prefectural level. The prefecture and county officials were assessed, appointed, and dismissed by the central government. Under the county level were the basic organization township and *Li* (administrative units of twenty-five neighboring households). Among the township officials, *Sanlao* was responsible for education, *Sefu* was responsible for case hearing and taxation, and *Youjiao* was responsible for public security.

The country governed the people and levied taxes through the three chief ministers and nine departments as well as through administrative organizations at various local levels. The individual household became the basic unit of society in the country.

In the economic sphere, Emperor Shihuang ordered landlords and yeomen who owned land to base both household registrations and taxes on actual land area occupied. Thus, private ownership of land was confirmed by law to protect the advanced landowner economy mode. Before the unification of the Qin Dynasty, the currencies of different vassal states had different shapes, sizes, and weights, and the measuring units were not the same, which hindered the development of nationwide commodity exchange and tax collection. In 221 BC, Emperor Shihuang unified the currency and weight and measure standards to strengthen regional economic ties. This encouraged ease in the exchange of goods and services, enhancing the country's economic unity.

Bronze weight of the Qin Dynasty. Engraved on its body are the characters for "eight *jin*" and the imperial decree for unifying the metrology, issued on the 26th year of the Qin Dynasty.

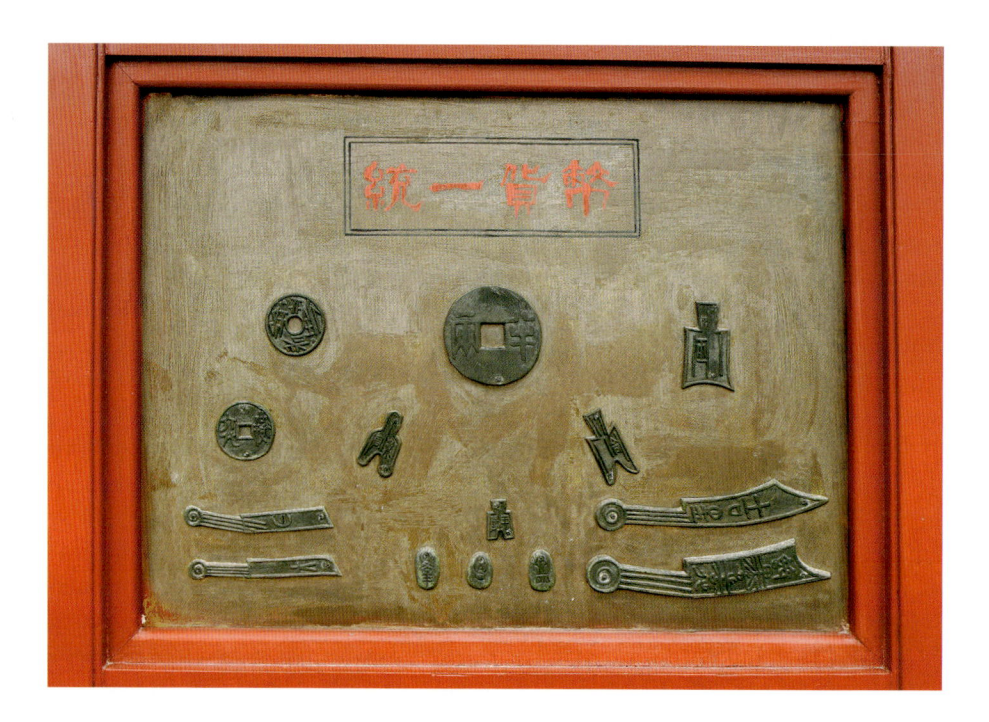

Upon unification by Emperor Shihuang of the Qin Dynasty, the spade-shaped coins, knife-shaped coins, and bronze shells circulated in previous kingdoms were unified into a round coin with a square hole.

After unification, the Qin removed barricades built by the six states, unified vehicle specifications, and built a network of roads centered around its capital, Xianyang (northeast of today's Xianyang, Shaanxi). In the course of conquering the Lingnan area (today's Guangdong and Guangxi provinces), the Lingqu Canal was dug to link the Yangtze River and the Pearl River systems. A wide valley road was built in the hills from today's Yibin, Sichuan, to Qujing, Yunnan. These measures ensured the smooth communication of political decrees and the ease of dispatching an army, promoted economic and cultural exchanges among the regions and ethnic groups, and forged a solid material foundation for a unified state.

Before unification, the Chinese language varied from state to state in terms of pronunciation and spelling. After unification, Emperor Shihuang made the *Xiaozhuan* (small seal character) the standard for the whole country. It helped in terms of communicating political decrees and cultural exchange, and greatly intensified the the people's sense of identification and belonging to a single Chinese culture. In the subsequent 2,000 years, written Chinese remained a unified form, and had a profound influence on the consolidation of a unified multiethnic country.

After unification, the Qin Dynasty also absorbed certain relevant rules and regulations of the former six states to formulate the legal system of Qin, which covered a wide range of laws, including criminal, procedure, civil, economic, and administrative.

In 213 BC, some conservative Confucians insisted that "no sustainable governance would be achieved without imitating ancient people and following long-established rules." Li Si firmly criticized those opponents. Emperor Shihuang accepted the suggestion of Li Si and further strengthened ideological control. He allowed public schools only, prohibited private schools, ordered the historiographers to burn historical records and all folk books, including *The Book of Odes, The Book of History,* and other books of all schools. He kept only

A tiger-shaped tally issued by Emperor Shihuang of the Qin Dynasty to generals stationed in Yangling. It is divided into two halves with a 12-character inscription on both parts saying, "the tally for troop movement with the emperor holding the right part and the generals in Yangling the left." The left and right halves must match each other for troop dispatch.

The History of Qin and books on medicine and forestation. He also ruled that those participating in private discussions on the *Book of Odes* and the *Book of History* would be executed, as would the entire family of those who questioned and criticized the government policy.

In 212 BC, some scholars and alchemists accused Emperor Shihuang of being "greedy for power" and "glad at severe penalty." More than 400 people were arrested and buried alive under the crime of defamation. Although the action of burning books and burying scholars alive suppressed opponents and safeguarded his centralized reign, the emperor's cruel manner caused a huge loss to the status of Chinese culture and had a negative political influence. Most wars and projects initiated by Emperor Shihuang were of progressive significance. However, the heavy taxation, the rigid penalties, the urgent deployment of men for his projects, and the construction of palaces and tombs, brought a heavy burden and suffering to the people. In 210 BC, Emperor Shihuang died of illness during a tour of inspection.

Emperor Ershi of the Qin Dynasty succeeded to the throne. The ruling classes were embroiled in internal discord, resulting in heavier taxation, more cruel punishment, and a rapidly intensifying social division. In 209 BC, a large-scale peasant uprising led by Chen Sheng and Wu Guang eupted, which heavily shook the rule of the Qin Dynasty. In 207 BC, the Qin Dynasty ended under the attack of Xiang Yu, Liu Bang, and other forces. After the four-year Chu-Han War, Liu Bang defeated Xiang Yu in 202 BC and set up the Han Dynasty in Chang'an (today's Xi'an), known in history as the Western Han Dynasty.

Though the Qin Dynasty ended only after the rule of two emperors, the new systems established by Emperor Shihuang made pioneering contributions to the development of China as a unified multiethnic country and took Chinese history on a new path in its following 2,000 years.

Western Han Dynasty's Strategies to Consolidate Centralized Rule

The tyranny and turmoil in the closing years of the Qin Dynasty left a shabby, jittery economy for the early Han Dynasty, whose rulers learned lessons from the collapse of the Qin and applied a policy of rehabilitation. During the period of Emperor Wendi and Jingdi, the economy recovered and society stabilized, resulting in the first peaceful period in Chinese ancient history.

Based on this, Emperors Wudi of the Han Dynasty abolished the tyranny of the Qin and continued its unifying and expansionary policy. Moreover, some adjustments and renewals were made, further consolidating the unified multiethnic country initiated by Qin.

Economically, the Han regime reduced taxes and the use of unpaid labor in exchange for taxes, and rewarded production. Liu Bang, Emperor Gaozu of the Han Dynasty, instigated a range of favorbale measures. He released soldiers to farm in the fields, offered amnesty for and enlisted refugees, freed servants and maids, exempted some and reduced the numbers of those doing unpaid labor, and set land rent at 1/15, resulting in a mass movement of population back into agricultural production.

Emperor Wendi used rates of agricultural and textile development to evaluate local officials and reduced the land rent to 1/30. These measures accelerated recovery and development of agriculture. Emperor Wudi further promoted the official monopoly of salt and iron, collected industrial and commercial taxes, established buffer institutions to control prices, unified the currency, prohibited private coin casting, and implemented other financial reforms. Thus, the country firmly stabilized the economy and increased financial income, laying a solid economic foundation for a unified empire.

As for the state regime, the Western Han Dynasty experienced its ups and downs. In the early Han Dynasty, Liu Bang rewarded some high-achieving ministers by granting them titles of vassals despite their family names being different from the royal one. Feudal and prefecture organizations coexisted. The area of seven vassals' fiefs equaled half of the territory of the Western Han Dynasty. They had their own troops and constituted a threat to the imperial power.

Liu Bang exterminated the vassals successively and subinfeudated his nephews. He hoped to rely on Liu's families to defend the borders. With the passing of time, the vassals of the same surname gradually became more powerful and did things in their own way. They established laws, collected taxes and tributes, and cast coins without permission from the central government. They became more wealthy than the emperor.

These vassals organized armed rebellions to challenge the central authority. Emperor Jingdi's acceptance of Minister Chao Cuo's suggestion to "remove monarchs" aroused the joint rebellion of Wu, Chu, and five other states. Emperor Jiingdi was forced to kill Chao Cuo to apologize to the seven states, but that didn't stop an attack from rebel forces. Finally, General Zhou Yafu defeated the rebels. After putting down the rebellions, the court revoked the vassals' power.

Emperor Wudi learned a lesson from the rebellion caused by feoffing and promulgated the "fief expansion order" for further distribution of fief to greatly reduce the vassals' might. He also divested 106 nobles of their rank at one sacrifice ceremony on the pretext that the gold they presented was of insufficient weight and poor quality.

Meanwhile, Emperor Wudi also strengthened imperial power by controlling both central and local administrative institutions. To do this, he promoted some middle and lower officials, who formed a "central court" to assist the emperor in decision-making, while an "outer court" led by the prime minister exclusively took care of political affairs. The supervision system was an important part of the centralized political system and was greatly strengthened in the Han Dynasty. Emperor Wudi established the position of *Silixiaowei* at the central level to supervise the behavior of officials and imperial members.

He also divided the country into thirteen supervision areas and sent one *Cishi* (provincial governor) to each area to inspect local officials and to curb and attack illegally rich people on behalf of the central government, thus enhancing the centralized regime.

The rulers of the Han Dynasty practiced the recommendation system. Local officials recommended talented people to the court, which appointed them according to their capabilities upon examination. The government enrolled people with special reputations and capabilities to officiate in the court, a process called *zheng* (enrollment). The practice under which a senior official recruited his subordinates was called *pi*. The official selection system attached more importance to the capabilities of the talents, but could easily be subverted by cronyism, giving rise to phenomena such as a recommended scholar who was unable to read, and a recommended *Xiaolian* (a role model of being filial to one's parents and clean as an official) who did not live with his parents.

Eaves tile saying "Han's dominance over China," unearthed from the Chang'an site, Xi'an, Shaanxi.

To avoid decades of governance by an official in a place that might result in corruption or set-up of a separate regime, the Han Dynasty set terms for major local officials; their origins and any blood relations with their superior leaders would be taken into consideration as well.

The prevalence of the quiet and inactive Taoism in the early Han Dynasty had created a rather liberal intellectual space, a departure from the growing centralization. The political situation during the reign of Emperor Wudi was stable, and national power was strong. Hence, ideological control was strengthened. Emperor Wudi adopted Dong Zhongshu's suggestion of "rejection of various philosophical schools and exclusive reverence of Confucianism." Confucianism, which propagated centralized rule, held the position of dominant official ideology. The policy penetrated into politics, ideology, culture, and education, helping to attack local regimes and consolidate centralization. It had a far-reaching influence by intensifying both Chinese culture and the monarch's control of popular thought.

The renovation measures concerning politics, economy, ideology, and other aspects implemented by Emperor Wudi, based on actual situations, proved quite fruitful and drove forward the development of the unified multiethnic country initiated by Qin.

Consolidating Northern Borders and Developing the Western Regions

The Qin and Han dynasties saw the rise of nomadic Huns living in the northern Mongolian Plateau. The oases west of Yumen Pass and Yangguan Pass, including present-day Xinjiang, Central Asia, and areas even further west, were called Western Regions, where "thirty-six kingdoms," including Wusun and Cheshi, were created.

The Huns, who conquered the Western Regions in the early Han Dynasty, confronted the Qin and Han dynasty forces along the natural north–south agricultural boundary between them. The relationship between both parties had a direct effect on the stability and development of the river bends, the Western Regions, and even the unified multiethnic country.

In 215 BC, General Meng Tian, dispatched by Emperor Shihuang of the Qin Dynasty, led 300,000 soldiers to attack the Huns, regaining the previously occupied river bends and establishing counties there. To defend against the Huns, the Qin Dynasty reinforced the old walls along the northern borders built by the former states of Yan, Zhao, and Qin. The effort resulted in the initial formation of the world famous Great Wall that extends from Lintao,

The site of Western Han's Great Wall at Yumen Pass, Dunhuang, Gansu.

Gansu, in the west to Liaodong in the east. Twelve prefectures were set up along the walls. The vast number of people who immigrated there to consolidate the border areas laid the foundation for stabilizing the northern borders and developing the Western Regions.

The early Han Dynasty saw a depressed economy and failures in its defensive wars against the Huns. Even peace-making marriages and bribery couldn't stop the Huns from achieving a large-scale intrusion. Relying on improved national strength, Emperor Wudi waged two great battles successively in places south and north of the Yellow River, driving the Huns out of the South Desert. He further sent Wei Qing and Huo Qubing to chase the Huns in the North Desert. Meanwhile, a vigorous effort was made to build walls along the areas west of the Yellow River, with beacon towers at short intervals extending west to Lop Nur in Xinjiang.

Before long, the Huns broke up into several groups. Huhanye, Khan of the Huns, led his troops to submit to the Han Dynasty and agreed that "the Han Dynasty and Hun are one family and no cheating or attacking is allowed." Emperor Yuandi of the Han Dynasty accepted the request of the Huns for a peace-making marriage and married Wang Zhaojun, a court lady, to Huhanye as a princess.

Zhaojun to the Border Area by Qiu Ying in the Ming Dynasty.

The unification of the Hun and Han peoples resulted in decades of peace and stability in the northern border areas. Consolidating borders with walls, reclaiming land, building roads, and increased bilateral trade all followed the peace-making marriages between the Han Dynasty and the Huns. This facilitated both social and economic development in the central plains, and helped spread advanced culture into the border areas.

Livestock in the early Han Dynasty were few, and officials had to travel in oxcarts. While under the regime of Emperor Wudi, areas south of the Great Wall saw "hordes of horses and cattle in fields." Livestock were used for farming and transportation, greatly enhancing productivity in the central plains. In the meantime, the Huns traded horses and cattle with inland merchants for daily necessities, which further spurred the development of a livestock economy.

Numerous unearthed cultural relics serve as proof that the iron plows, currencies used, and weighing and measuring instruments employed in such areas

Fresco from the tomb of the Han Dynasty in Helinge'er, Inner Mongolia, depicts the farming life of the northern nomadic people at the time.

as Gansu, Ordos of Inner Mongolia, and Liaoyang of Northeast China differed little from those adopted in inland areas.

The Han exploitation of the Western Regions is best showcased by the development of the Silk Road. It began in Chang'an, ran through the Hexi Corridor and present-day Xinjiang, to Central and West Asia, and finally to Europe. Along the land route that spanned the Asian and European continents, techniques of casting iron, digging wells, and making iron plows, and the concepts of plowing with oxen, raising silkworms, and reeling silk, as well as large quantities of metal tools and silk fabrics were transported from east to west, speeding the social progress of western areas. In return, the Akhal-Teke breed of horses, camels, fur goods, grapes, megranate fruit, benne (sesame), walnuts, and other products of the Western Regions, as well as wonderful foreign music and dances, were introduced to inland areas, blowing a fresh breath into to traditional Chinese culture.

The Silk Road also connected the Han Dynasty with countries of ancient civilization, such as Kushan, Arsacid, and Rome. In the 1st century BC, the Roman emperor Caesar once wore a "coat of Heaven" made of Chinese silk, and the Europeans called the Han Dynasty "Seres," meaning "the country of silk." Plinius, a Roman natural historian, mentioned in his book *Natural History* that, "despite the variety of iron, none equaled the iron from China (the Han Dynasty)." Furthermore, the Buddhism of ancient India, the art of ancient Rome, and various foreign sculptures and paintings were introduced from west to east. The opening of the Asia-Europe passageway, called the Silk Road by later generations, tightly connected the Western Regions with the central plains

Piece of a Dunhuang fresco: Zhang Qian bids farewell to Emperor Wudi of the Han Dynasty.

and produced a far-reaching influence on cultural exchanges between east and west and the development of human civilization.

The territory under Emperor Wudi, twice as large as that of the Qin Dynasty, supporting a population of 60 million at the peak of his rule. The establishment of such a vast and populous empire required mature political and economic systems, efficient management, harmonious relationships

Gold coin of the Eastern Roman Empire, unearthed along the Silk Road.

between the central and local governments and among ethnic groups, and a concentrated power based on consistent cultural concepts and values. Although territories changed, dynasties were replaced, and regime divisions and mergers were constant occurrences, the grand trend of unity was never reversed.

At the end of the Western Han Dynasty, Wang Mang, a relative of the emperor on his wife's side, seized power and crowned himself in 9 AD, starting the Xin Dynasty that eventually replaced the Western Han. But, fourteen years later, insurgent peasant armies *Lulin* (Greenwoods) and *Chimei* (Red Eyebrow) captured Chang'an and exterminated Xin. In 25 AD, Liu Xiu resumed the Han Dynasty in Luoyang, known as the Eastern Han Dynasty. Liu Xiu released servants and maids and reduced taxation. The society and economy recovered and developed. The power of the local despots he relied on expanded accordingly. At the end of the Eastern Han Dynasty, eunuchs and the relatives of the emperor on his wife's side controlled the court. Struggle and strife led to social turbulence, and under the onslaught of the *Huangjin* (Yellow Turban) Peasant Uprising, imperial power declined and fell into the hands of scattered warlords. In 220 AD, Cao Pi dethroned Emperor Xiandi of the Han Dynasty and established the Wei Dynasty in Luoyang, marking the end of the Eastern Han.

Booming Culture of the Qin and Han Dynasties

The establishment of a unified country paved the way for sustainable cultural growth. The Qin and Han dynasties witnessed further advances in science and culture. The invention of paper is China's most prominent contribution to human civilization. Chinese characters first appeared on pottery, tortoise shells, and bronze ware, and later on bamboo slips and silk cloth, all of which were either heavy or expensive and made cultural communication difficult.

In the early Western Han Dynasty, workmen, while beating pods into silk, found that characters could be written on the remaining silk membranes. Enlightened by the process, the Chinese people adopted flax as a raw material to produce the earliest plant fiber paper, which was still rough and not suitable for writing. In the Eastern Han Dynasty, the eunuch Cai Lun resorted to tree bark, flax cloth, rags, old fishing nets, and other readily available raw materials to make a high quality yet inexpensive paper called "Marquis Cai Paper." From then on, paper was produced on a large scale and became the most popular material for writing.

Chapter 4 The Qin and Han Dynasties   **67**

A hemp paper map from the Western Han Dynasty, unearthed in Fangmatan, Tianshui, Gansu.

China's paper-making technique was first exported to Korea and Vietnam, then to Japan in the 7th century, to Arabian counties in the 8th century, and to Europe in the 12th century. Paper played a significant role in worldwide communication, education, and trade, and had a profound impact on the progress of world civilization.

The iron-smelting sector of the Han Dynasty remained as advanced as before. Quenching techniques were invented and coal was used as a fuel for

A bronze galloping horse from the Eastern Han Dynasty, unearthed in Wuwei, Gansu.

Pottery Boat of the Eastern Han Dynasty, unearthed in Guangzhou, Guangdong.

smelting. In the Eastern Han Dynasty, wind power was used to smelt metal, and a low-temperature steel-making technique was invented and popularized. With regard to ship-building, more efficient sculls, more flexible stern steering wheels, cloth sails that relied on wind power, and more firm anchors were invented, leading to improved navigation techniques.

In the handicraft sector, the superb black porcelains made in the late Eastern Han Dynasty marked the maturity of porcelain-making techniques first initiated in China. Improved silk embroidery workmanship resulted in more diverse categories of embroidery. Their exquisite patterns and bright colors enabled them to be exported to East Asia and Europe in large quantities and were reputed by the Romans to be "the world's number one fabric."

With regard to the measurement of celestial bodies, Zhang Heng of the Eastern Han Dynasty invented the earliest "armillary sphere" (instrument with rings showing the positions of heavenly bodies) that revolved with hydraulic power. He also invented a seismograph that could precisely measure the direction of earthquakes thousands of miles away—more than 1,700 years earlier than similar devices invented in Europe.

Unlike Greek classical mathematics that focused on theorem proving, ancient Chinese mathematics focused on the creation of algorithms, especially those that solved equations. The *Zhou Bi Mathematical Manual* written in the

Chapter 4 The Qin and Han Dynasties 69

Seismograph invented by Zhang Heng (model).

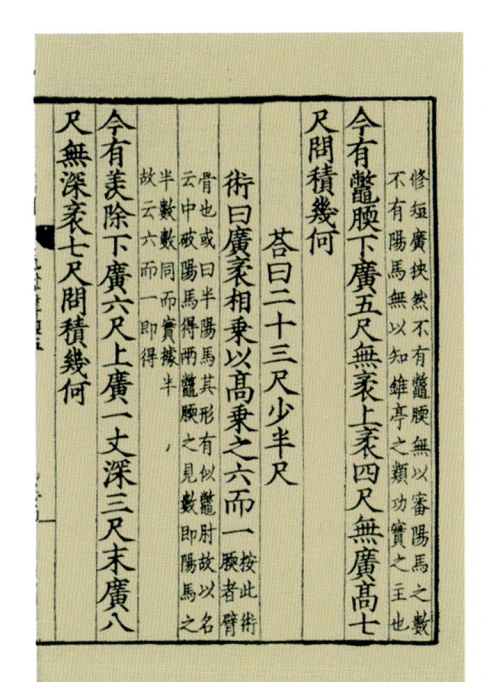

Page from Liu Hui's *The Nine Chapters on Mathematical Art*.

Western Han Dynasty first records a special case in geometry known as the Pythagorean Theorem, about 500 years earlier than that proposed in the west.

The *Nine Chapters on Mathematical Art* written during the Eastern Han Dynasty was a collection of mathematical achievements from pre-Qin to the Han Dynasty, and was respected as the most important book of its kind. The book records all the algorithms for practical problems closely related to production, such as those relevant to land areas, grain, trade, warehouse size, earthworks, and tax, and those that summarize ways of calculating positive and negative numbers, plus ways to solve quadratic equations. Its presence marked the formation of the ancient Chinese mathematical system in which counting rods were used as the calculation tool, and the decimal system was adopted.

The *Nine Chapters on Mathematical Art* was introduced to Japan in the Sui and Tang dynasties, and some parts of the book spread to India and the Arab world, and even to Europe.

Many famous doctors and classic books emerged in the Han Dynasty. The Yellow Emperor's *Classic of Internal Medicine* written during the Western Han is a pioneering book of traditional Chinese medical theory. The book, in two parts, has 162 articles in eighteen volumes. It discusses basic theories concerning the body, physiology, causes of disease, and diagnosis, as well as acupuncture, channels and collaterals, and health care.

Portrait of Hua Tuo.

Emperor Shen Nong's *Materia Medica,* written during the Eastern Han Dynasty, is a summary of medicines used since the Warring States Period, and became the foundation for subsequent Chinese pharmacology. Zhang Zhongjing, known as the "Medicine Saint" in the Eastern Han Dynasty, proposed a set of traditional Chinese theories in *The Treatise on Febrile Diseases,* including the three causes of disease and treatment according to syndrome differentiation. Hua Tuo, a highly skilled doctor in the Eastern Han, invented *Mafeisan,* the earliest surgical anesthetic, performed the first abdominal cavity operation in China, and invented the five-animal frolics.

Against the backdrop of unification, the official mainstream ideology in the Qin and Han dynasties experienced a transformation from "contention of a hundred schools of thought" to "paying supreme tribute to one thought while banning all other schools of thought." The legalist thought of the Warring States period was adopted by Emperor Yingzheng as a sharp tool for pushing reform; through abandoning Confucianism and absorbing part of the diverse thoughts of many schools, it further became the dominant ideology guiding the politics of the Qin Dynasty after unification.

In the early western Han Dynasty, the economy was seriously damaged and a host of neglected tasks cried for attention. Faced with a need to rehabilitate the economy, the intellectual field was relatively open, and the philosophy of Huang Di and Lao Tze prevailed. During the reign of Emperor Wudi, ideological control intensified as the political situation became more stable and the economy prospered. Confucianist Dong Zhongshu put forward the opinion of "paying supreme tribute to Confucianism while

Stone Carving of the Han Dynasty: Sermon.

banning all other schools of thought" and "banning all ways of spreading other schools of thought" except Confucianism, which he believed could make the people know how to behave and who to obey, and thus safeguard the imperial power. Emperor Wudi accepted his suggestion and established it as a national strategy.

The new Confucianism of Dong Zhongshu, was in fact, a new ideological system shaped by combining many schools of thought—the Yin-Yang School, Taoism, and Legalism based on Confucius' political outlook of maintaining the hierarchical system, and the thought of unification highlighted in *The Kung-Yang Commentary on the Spring and Autumn Annals*. Dong Zhongshu claimed that "social norms originate in nature, and no changes in social norms shall happen without changes in nature." He advocated that "regality is awarded by heaven," based on the theory of "induction between heaven and man." He also warned that if the emperor was brutal in his rule, the heaven would send calamities to condemn and deter him. Therefore, the emperor must observe the way of the heaven and exercise benevolent rule. Dong emphasized that the emperor should rule the country with benevolence at its core and punishment as supplement, and put forward the ethical norms of benevolence, righteousness, propriety, wisdom, and fidelity. The three cardinal guides—the ruler guides his subjects; the father guides his son; and the husband guides his wife—were cardinal relationships that could not be changed.

"Paying supreme tribute to Confucianism while banning all other schools of thought" is an important event in the history of China. Confucianism's dominant position in politics was conducive to consolidating the unified country and stabilizing the social order. Confucianism became a required course in all schools and was the court's standard of assessment when selecting officials. Thus was the dominant position of Confucianism established in the traditional culture of China.

The *Records of the Grand Historian* written by Sima Qian, and *The Book of Han* written by Ban Gu are two famous historical books. Sima Qian, once the Prefect of the Grand Scribes and Chief of the Secretariat during the regime of Emperor Wudi, compiled China's first general history. He assembled parts of previous historical books and the thought of many schools, made use of files collected by the State, and conducted field investigations and interviews. The book includes 130 chapters and more than 500,000 words, recording all major historical events during the 3,000 years from the legendary Huangdi to Emperor Wudi.

The *Records of the Grand Historian* marked a fresh start in documenting historical events, systems, human activities, and social changes. It combines multiple ways of recording, including *Benji* (biographical sketches of kings),

Portrait of Sima Qian.

Biao (tables), *Shu* (records of systems), *Shijia* (records of vassals), and *Liezhuan* (biographies), becoming the model for subsequent Chinese historians.

The *Book of Han* written by Ban Gu was the first book of dynastic history, offering detailed and in-depth descriptions about the social evolution of the Han Dynasty.

The achievements of literature in the Han Dynasty were best reflected in the creation of *Fu* and *Yuefu*. Fu is a rhymed prose style that combines the rational spirit of *The Book of Odes* prior to the Qin Dynasty with the romantic expression of the Chu odes. Fu attaches importance to expatiation, parallelism, and ornate language. Sima Xiangru and Yang Xiong were the most notable writers of Fu.

Yuefu was a musical department established during the reign of Emperor Wudi of the Han Dynasty. Poems collected, sorted, and recorded by the Yuefu department were called Yuefu poetry, which inherited and developed the excellent tradition of the folk songs in *The Book of Odes* with lively language and various forms.

The Terracotta Warriors and Horses of Emperor Shihuang of the Qin Dynasty showcase the outstanding artistic achievements of the Qin and Han dynasties with their exquisite artistic shapes and spectacular scale.

Terracotta warriors and horses escorting the Mausoleum of Emperor Shihuang of the Qin Dynasty.

Nearly 10,000 terracotta warriors and horses have been found. The same size as real ones, all have different expressions and lively postures. The 14,000-square-meter No.1 pit holds a huge army: 6,000 terracotta warriors and horses, more than 40 chariots, and 160 war-horses. The army is "marching" eastward with the momentum of an avalanche, like a living army, reproducing the gallant manner of the Qin troops that bravely fought against the other six states in the central plains, manifesting the pioneering spirit of the time and the grandness of a unified empire.

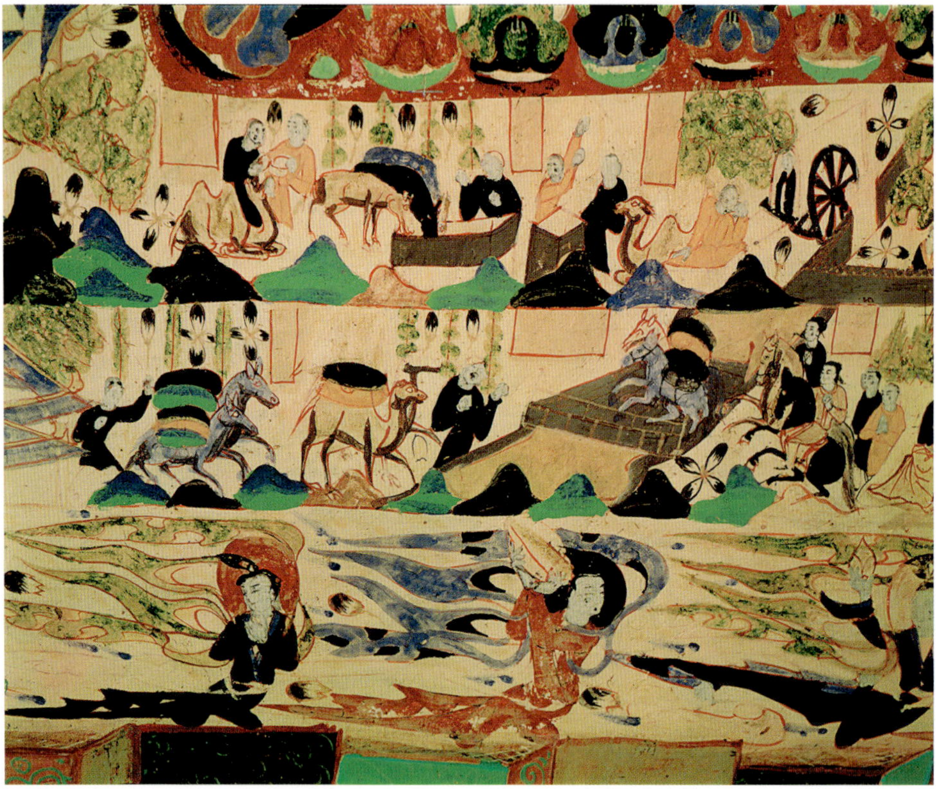

Chapter 5

The Wei, Jin, and Southern and Northern Dynasties: Regime Division and Ethnic Concentration

The Three Kingdoms Period and the Southern and Northern Dynasties

The period from 220 AD to 589 AD witnessed the rise and fall of the Wei, Jin, and Southern and Northern Dynasties. A turbulent political situation, the multiple struggles for domination, and the entry of northern ethnic groups into the central plains resulted in long-tem disunity of the country and confrontation between south and north.

The main reason for the struggles among local warlords was the malignant expansion of local despots since the Eastern Han Dynasty. Upon the establishment of the Eastern Han, Liu Xiu greatly rewarded both ministers and relatives. Some famed families monopolized key offices of the court for several generations. They greedily annexed land by means of political privilege and set up manors nationwide. Bankrupted and exiled peasants were forced to attach themselves to the despots and landlords as tenant peasants.

Using their political privileges, these powerful households tyrannized the society. They had economic power over tenant peasants. They built high walls, moats, and private armed forces. Seizing the opportunity of a turbulent situation, they crazily expanded their power, spawning warlord groups that monopolized local areas and initiated wars against others. The final result was the rise of three powers, known as Caowei, Shuhan, and Sunwu.

Cao Cao was once a Commander of Military Standards during the reign of Emperor Lingdi at the end of the Han Dynasty. He participated in the

Chibi. The War at Chibi was decisive to the formation of the Three Kingdoms.

allied troop crusade against the rebellious minister Dong Zhuo. Cao Cao later defeated the Yellow Turbans at Qingzhou, incorporated more than 300,000 soldiers into his troops, and further established a valiant army called Qingzhou Troops. In 196 AD, Cao Cao took back Emperor Xiandi, who had been held under duress by Dong Zhuo, and moved the capital to Xuxian (present-day Xuchang, Henan), gaining a favorable position of "coercing the emperor to control all his vassals." In 200 AD, he won the battle at Guandu against the troops of Yuan Shao and gained control over areas both north and south of the Yellow River.

Cao Cao further conquered Wuhuan of Liaoxi, which basically unified the northern part of China. In 208 AD, he led a troop southward but was defeated by the allied army of Sun Quan and Liu Bei at Chibi, resulting in a pattern of the whole country being controlled by three regimes. Retreating to the north, Cao Cao successively occupied Guanzhong and Liangzhou and expanded the scope of his power in the northwestern areas. Politically, Cao Cao respected the wise and believed talent was the only criterion for selecting officials. He also beefed up the centralized rule and attacked those who were getting rich or powerful through illegal means. Economically, he prohibited land mergers, and implemented the *Tuntian* System (a kind of government-encouraged agricultural system) and the *Zudiao* System (a tax system). He recruited exiled peasants to reclaim barren land on a large scale. These efforts greatly promoted the development of the northern economy, which had been damaged by ceaseless wars, and helped widespread areas of desolate fields morph into a land of harvest and abundance. After Cao Cao's death in 220 AD, Cao Pi dethroned Emperor Xiandi and established the Wei Dynasty, historically called Caowei.

Chapter 5   The Wei, Jin, and Southern and Northern Dynasties

Liu Bei was a descendant of the royal family of the Han Dynasty. After the family fortunes declined in his early years, he went to his relative, Liu Biao, the governor of Jinzhou, for help. As a man of ambition, Liu Bei always sought positions of power and control and went everywhere to find those who could assist him. It is said he once paid three visits to a thatched cottage in Longzhong, Jinzhou, to engage Zhuge Liang. Following the death of Liu Biao, Liu Bei controlled Jinzhou. In 211 AD, he attacked Hanzhong and further occupied Yizhou in Sichuan, consolidating his rule over the southwestern region. In 221 AD, Liu Bei declared himself a descendant of the former imperial family and established a state, historically called Shuhan, with Chengdu as its capital. Assisted by Prime Minister Zhuge Liang, Liu Bei implemented clean politics and paid particular attention to the state's relationship with local ethnic groups. Economically, he also made a vigorous effort to popularize raising silkworms, to develop iron smelting, and to encourage textile and other handicraft sectors, leading to the rapid development of the southwestern regions and close ties with the central plains.

Terracotta officials or soldiers of the Western Jin Dynasty, unearthed in Changsha, Hunan.

Ladies' Outing, brick carving of the Southern Dynasties.

Sun Quan, who relied on rich and powerful landlords and inherited his family fortunes in areas south of the Yangtze, was confronted with Caowei across the Yangtze and rapidly expanded in areas south of the river. He later drove the forces of Liu Bei from Jingzhou and occupied Lingnan, extending his scope of power southeastward. In 229 AD, Sun Quan ascended the throne, established Jianye (present-day Nanjing) as the capital, and changed the state tile to Wu, historically called Sunwu.

Wei, Shu, and Wu each achieved regional unification, respectively making significant contributions to local social progress. Caowei was the strongest of all. Upon Zhuge Liang's death, the Shuhan regime was monopolized by eunuchs, resulting in political corruption and waning national strength. Caowei finally eliminated the regime in 263 AD. After Emperor Mingdi of Caowei died, minister Sima Yan seized the regime and, in 266 AD, came into power and changed the state title to Jin, historically called the Western Jin. In the later period of Sunwu, the tyrannical and extravagant Emperor Sun Hao aroused widespread complaints and anger among the people. In 280 AD, the Western Jin ended Sunwu, thereby unifying the whole country. Due to bureaucratic corruption, the Rebellion of Eight Princes and the consequent sharpened class contradictions and ethnic conflicts, the Western Jin lasted for only thirty years and was ended by the northern ethnic regime in 316. In 317, the remaining royal family of the Western Jin moved to areas south of the Yangtze and established Jiankang (present-day Nanjing, Jiangsu) as the capital of the state, historically called Eastern Jin, which lasted about 100 years.

Chapter 5 The Wei, Jin, and Southern and Northern Dynasties

In 420 AD, Liu Yu overthrew the Eastern Jin and changed the state title to Song. From then on, the areas south of the Yangtze witnessed frequent changes of regimes from Song (420–479), to Qi (479–502), to Liang (502–557), and to Chen (557–589), collectively called the Southern Dynasties in Chinese history.

A dozen ethnic regimes took root in the north from 304, generally called the Sixteen States Period. In 439, the Northern Wei, led by the Tuobas from the Xianbei ethnic group, unified the Yellow River Valley. Later on, after divisions and replacements, the Eastern Wei (534–550), the Northern Qi (550–577), the Western Wei (535–556), and the Northern Zhou (557–581) stood out and were called the Northern Dynasties. The Northern and Southern Dynasties confronted each other and are collectively called the Southern and Northern Dynasties.

Drastic social turmoil and long-term wars led to national division, economic decline, and destruction of the social fabric. After more than three centuries of chaos, many northern ethnic groups gradually merged with one another during the regime conflicts and exchanges. The southern areas experienced unprecedented economic development and laid a solid foundation for subsequent reunification.

Development of Areas South of the Yangtze

Due to ecological diversity in ancient China, three major economic zones—the stockbreeding zone north of Jieshi, Longmen; the traditional agricultural zone in the central plains in the Yellow River basins; and the areas south of the Yangtze—took shape as early as the Qin and Han dynasties. Different regions had distinctive economic features that complemented one another. The central plains, including present-day Henan, Shandong, and Hebei, as well as southern Shanxi, northern Jiangsu, and northern Anhui, enjoyed superior natural conditions and were developed earlier. The region is home to Chinese civilization and has long been the economic center of China. While areas south of the Yangtze, with hot, wet weather and widespread forests and wetlands, saw the dominance of hunting, fishing, and lumbering.

In the Qin and Han dynasties, parts of the area south of the Yangtze were preliminarily developed, while areas like Chuyue still featured vast land and a sparsely distributed population. But the backward situation was soon changed in the Eastern Jin and Southern Dynasties, as the national economic center started to move southward.

The Wei and Jin dynasties experienced the second period of freezing weather in ancient China. Wars, excessive reclamation, and freezing weather rapidly destroyed agricultural ecology in the Yellow River Valley. In contrast,

Ox-cart, brick carving from the Southern Dynasties.

areas south of the Yangtze showed a huge potential for economic development with better weather conditions and abundant resources.

After moving southward, the Western Jin effectively prevented the invasion of northern nomads by relying on the natural moat of the Yangtze. In 383, an 800,000-soldier troop of the *Di* ethnic group marched southward, but was defeated by the 80,000-soldier troop of the Eastern Jin, which resolutely waged a counterattack at Feishui. The soldiers saved the area south of the Yangtze from invasion, providing a relatively stable environment for local economic development.

The Rebellion of Eight Princes in the Western Jin Dynasty and the immigration of northern nomads to inland areas led to decades of chaos in northern China and large-scale southward migration from the central plains.

During the 170 years from the end of the Western Jin to the early Southern dynasties, up to 900,000 people moved to the south, one-sixth of its total population. This migration helped import both labor and advanced tools and production techniques southward, offering a powerful impetus to the economic growth south of the Yangtze. Stretches of barren land were reclaimed, and many water conservancy projects were constructed. Iron plows drawn by oxen were adopted, and a crop system combining paddy rice and wheat planting was created. Craftsmen also moved from north to south on a large scale, helping create a boom in the handicraft sector. Silk weaving, iron smelting, and pottery works enhanced the prosperity of commerce in the cities. According to *The Book of the Song Dynasty,* the southern area became the most prosperous place in the country during the Eastern Jin and

Southern dynasties. Ancient China's economic center started to shift from the northern Yellow River Valley to the southern Yangtze River's middle and lower reaches.

Gathering of Northern Ethnic Groups

The relationship between the northern ethnic groups and the Han group is an important factor in Chinese history. Since the time of the Eastern Han Dynasty, the northern and northwestern ethnic groups, like the Huns, Xianbei, Jie, Di, and Qiang, had been forced to move into the hinterlands and become tenant peasants, soldiers, or even servants, further sharpening the divisions between ethnic groups. Some ethnic regimes were set up during the struggle against the Han rulers. These groups continuously advanced to the central plains when the Han reign was under duress.

At the time of the Wei and Jin dynasties, the northern ethnic groups' migration resulted in a "half population in northwestern prefectures." In the midst of great chaos, they kept their original clan organization and set up ethnic regimes. They revolted against oppression, strengthened their power, struggled for wealth, and attacked one another, intensifying social turbulence and wars. On the other hand, the ethnic groups were registered as national households mainly engaged in agriculture. They lived together and married local people. The frequent exchanges resulted in a general trend of harmony.

After decades of living together through thick and thin, most ethnic groups acknowledged the culture of the central plains, regarding themselves offspring of Yandi and Huangdi. Most imitated the political and economic policies of the central plains that had developed to varying degrees since the

Harrowing land, brick carving of the Wei and Jin dynasties.

Messenger, mural of the Wei and Jin dynasties.

Han and Wei dynasties. For instance, Liu Yuan, an aristocrat of Hun, was well acquainted with classical works on Confucianism as well as with *The Records of the Grand Historian, The Book of Han,* and *The Art of War.* He claimed himself the nephew of the emperor of the Han Dynasty and established a state with the title of Han. His successor, Liu Cong, was equally acquainted with literature and history and was good at calligraphy, capable of cursive handwriting and official script, and wrote hundreds of poems and odes. Fu Jian of the Pre-Qin Dynasty declared his intent to "mix all the ethnic groups into one family." He attached great importance to Han Chinese officials, courteously treated distinguished persons of all ethnic groups, and worked to popularize Confucianism and the systems of the Han Chinese in an all-around way. After the Northern Wei built by the Xianbei ethnic group unified the north, ethnic group acculturation sped up.

At the beginning of the Northern Wei reunification, many outdated traditions were still in existence. For instance, in war, the infantries for assault were composed of Han Chinese and other ethnic groups, while the Xianbei cavalries supervised them from behind. This and other forms of social injustice aroused intense resistance.

Queen Mother Feng, a Han Chinese who grew up in the central plains culture, prompted Tuoba Hong, Emperor Xiaowendi of the Northern Wei, who succeeded to the throne at five, to reform.

To smoothly promote reform and better learn the culture of the central plains, Emperor Xiaowendi moved his capital from the remote Ping Cheng

Emperor Xiaowendi dressed in Han clothes on an imperial inspection, discovered in Longmen Grottoes, Luoyang.

(today's Datong, Shanxi) to Luoyang, which became the capital for several dynasties. After the move, he greatly promoted the Han Chinese-oriented policies, government organization, rituals, and codes. For life and customs, Ethnic-style clothes and Xianbei language were prohibited. Xianbei persons were to adapt their surnames per the Han Chinese style. He also advocated marriage between the Xianbei and the Han Chinese, and forbade marriage between Xianbei persons of the same surname.

During the reform, Emperor Xiaowendi set himself as an example to others by changing his royal surname from "Tuoba" to "Yuan" and renamed himself "Yuan Hong." He also married the daughter of a Han Chinese minister and married his daughter to a Chinese man. These all-around reforms in politics, economy, culture, and customs accelerated the the blending of ethnic groups into the Han Chinese culture.

Not only did the southern economy achieve an unprecedented boom, the northern ethnic groups gradually gathered together in the conflicts and were

Dunhuang fresco of the Northern Zhou Dynasty, documenting a highly active business scene business scene along the Silk Road.

converted by the civilization of the central plains. Without disturbing landlords who occupied land, the System of Equal Distribution of Land practiced in the Northern Wei area distributed land to peasants according to household population. That properly solved the problem of matching land and labor, and significantly pushed forward the means of production in the central plains, having a far-reaching influence on Chinese history.

Ethnic food, clothing, beds, music, and dances, all with the unique features of northern ethnic groups, as well as other advanced techniques of livestock breeding, disease prevention, and medical treatment, were gradually merged into the daily life of the Han Chinese, enriching the culture of the central plains. The ethnic group acculturation, epitomized by Emperor Xiaowendi's reform, laid a solid foundation for a deepened national reunification.

During the Wei, Jin, and Southern and Northern dynasties, the non-Chinese world also experienced a huge change. The Gupta Empire rose in India. The Arsacid Dynasty was ended by the Persian Empire. The brilliant ancient culture of Rome was interrupted by the invasion of other countries. Chinese culture continued and developed along a winding way, though experiencing prolonged disunity and wars.

Colorful and Diverse Culture in the Wei, Jin, and Southern and Northern Dynasties

The extension and development of Chinese culture during the period were also reflected in science, technology, and culture. Agronomy, medicine, mathematics, geology, calligraphy, painting, and sculpture surpassed those of the Qin and Han dynasties.

The period saw the invention of a method used to produce steel by combining pig iron and wrought iron, the creation of the rotating water cart, a highly efficient tool for irrigation, as well as the cultivation of a superior silkworm breed that could produce pods eight times a year. In addition, oil and natural gas were used for lighting, and even to create fire in an attack.

The book *Essential Techniques for the Peasantry,* written by Jia Sixie in the Wei State, systematically summarizes the experiences in farming, raising stock, fishing, and other production activities in the middle and lower reaches of the Yellow River, as well as the ways they processed and stored food. It is the first complete agricultural book in China, and is the world's first agricultural encyclopedia.

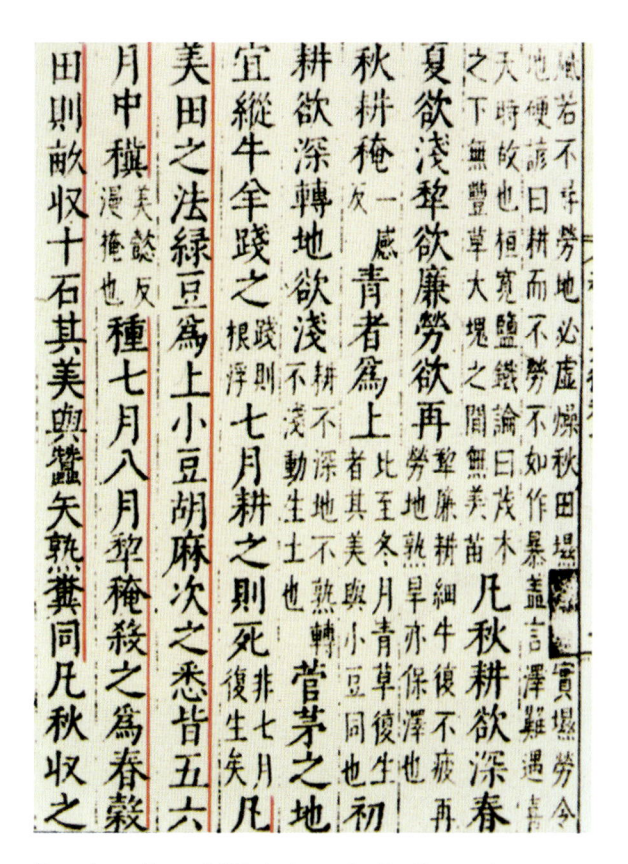

Chapter 5   The Wei, Jin, and Southern and Northern Dynasties

Page from *Essential Techniques for the Peasantry.*

The *Commentary on the Waterways Classic,* written by geographer Li Daoyuan, is a book of notes on previous works. Using more than 300,000 words, it goes into detail about 1,250 rivers as well as the mountains, landscapes, evolution of counties, local products, customs, history, and legends in areas along the waterways. The *Commentary on the Waterways Classic* is more than an excellent comprehensive geographical work; it is also of great significance in literature.

Zu Chongzhi, a mathematician in the Southern Dynasty, concluded that the value of pi falls between 3.1415926 and 3.1415927, an achievement preceding the West by 1,000 years. He formulated the Daming Calendar, concluding that a year actually includes 365.24281481 days, with an error of no more than 50 seconds. Zu Chongzhi was also good at making mechanical instruments, successfully duplicating the compass cart, even though its creation techniques had been lost for generations. Zu also created water mills, and a "thousand-*li*

Portrait of Zu Chongzhi.

ship" that could travel hundreds of *li* per day. In the 1960s, to commemorate his great contributions to world science and culture, the International Astronomical Union named a ring mountain on the moon as the "Mountain of Zu Chongzhi."

The collapse of the Eastern Han and the ensuing severe turbulence destroyed the overwhelming supremacy of Confucianism and led to a flourishing of legalism and metaphysics. Taoism and Buddhism introduced between the Western and Eastern Han dynasties were particularly prosperous, posing a challenge to the Confucianism that indulged in absurd arguments and dogmas.

The metaphysics that emerged between the Wei and Jin dynasties respected Lao Tze and Zhuang Tzu, and advocated "void is the nature of everything" and "acting in accordance with natural laws." Its representatives, such as Ji Kang and Ruan Ji, brazenly declared that "they despise King Tang of the Shang Dynasty and King Wu of the Zhou Dynasty, and belittle Zhougong and Confucius," both speaking and behaving beyond established ritual and legal norms. Metaphysics grew as the dominant school of thought at that time, driving forward the development of philosophical thinking and the liberation of individuals.

Buddhism, introduced into the central plains from ancient India during the Western and Eastern Han dynasties, prospered in the Wei and Jin dynasties. Buddhism emphasizes karma and samsara. Buddhists told people they could attain happiness in their afterlife, even when they had to tolerate pain in the current life, so long as they earnestly kept up Buddhist practices. Buddhist doctrines allowed maintenance of the hierarchical order, offered converts spiritual support, and were particularly attractive to the poor, who were struggling in the turbulent world of the time.

The Southern and Northern dynasties witnessed the peak of Buddhism in China. As the poems of Du Fu, a poet of the Tang Dynasty, described, "As many as 480 temples in the Southern and Northern dynasties are shrouded in mist and drizzle." In the Northern Dynasties, the number of Buddhist temples increased to more than 30,000, and monks and nuns to three million. The spread of Buddhism injected fresh elements and had a huge impact on traditional Chinese culture in such aspects as ideology, culture, art, and literature.

Taoism, established at the end of the Eastern Han Dynasty, is a native religion of China combining Taoist thought and supernatural art. Reconstructed by Ge Hong in the Eastern Jin Dynasty, it was lifted to an official position. Taoism advocates harmony between heaven and human beings, attainment of the highest state of spiritual enlightenment, and becoming immortal through self-cultivation and making of the immortality pills according to the Taoist doctrine. Tao Hongjing of the Southern Dynasties further established a system of immortals, ranging from the Jade Emperor to the City God and Kitchen God, which had a far-reaching influence upon ancient Chinese people.

The successive rise of metaphysics, Buddhism, and Taoism greatly destabilized Confucianism, creating an open, diverse and lively atmosphere in the ideological world, which led to competition among Confucianism, Buddhism, and Taoism.

The Wei, Jin, and Southern and Northern dynasties saw social turbulence and the collapse of ritual norms, which gave rise to calligraphy as an ideal form for scholars to express their thoughts and pursuits. Chinese character writing gradually evolved into a self-conscious calligraphic art. Wang Xizhi of the Eastern Jin Dynasty was known as the Sage of Calligraphers and his calligraphy featured fine brush strokes and aesthetically pleasing handwriting, bringing to mind the image of floating clouds or a flying dragon . His *Preface to the Orchid Pavilion,* which represents the pinnacle of the calligraphic art in the Jin Dynasty, is known as the "best running-hand work."

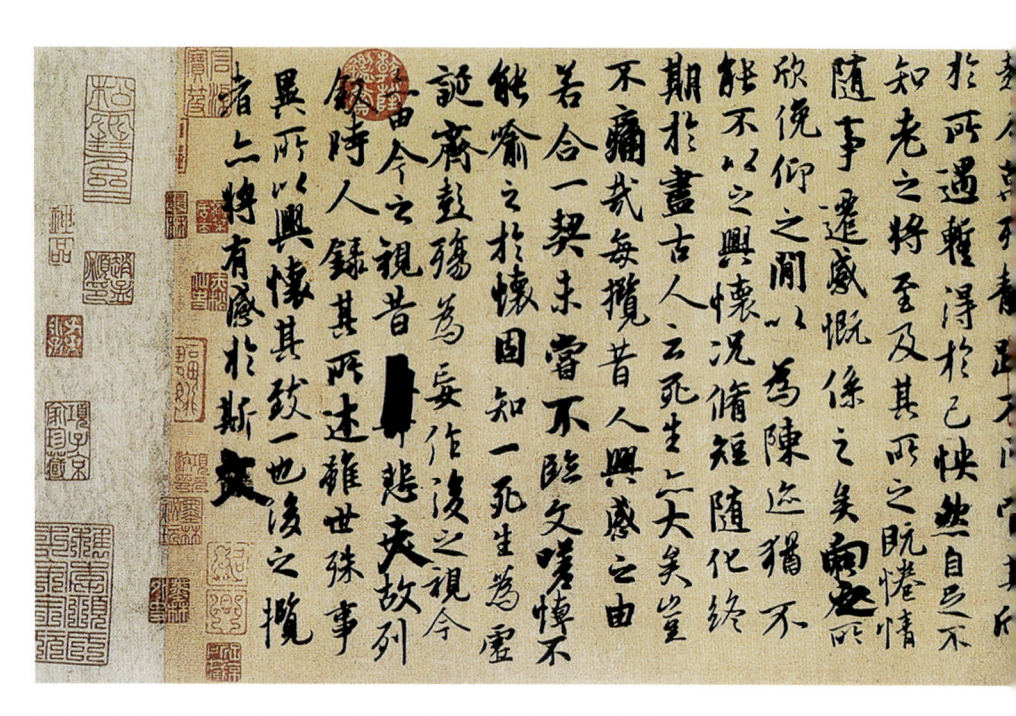

Preface to the Orchid Pavilion by Wang Xizhi of the Eastern Jin Dynasty.

Ode to the Goddess of Luo (part) by Gu Kaizhi in the Eastern Jin Dynasty.

永和九年歲在癸丑暮春之初會
于會稽山陰之蘭亭脩禊事
也群賢畢至少長咸集此地
有崇山峻領茂林脩竹又有清流激
湍暎帶左右引以為流觴曲水
列坐其次雖無絲竹管弦之
盛一觴一詠亦足以暢敘幽情
是日也天朗氣清惠風和暢仰
觀宇宙之大俯察品類之盛
所以遊目騁懷足以極視聽之
娛信可樂也夫人之相與俯仰
一世或取諸懷抱悟言一室之內
或因寄所託放浪形骸之外雖

Yungang Grottoes (located at Datong, Shanxi). Carving of the grottoes started in the second year of the Xing'an Period, Northern Wei and was largely completed before the dynasty's capital relocation to Luoyang.

The Wei and Jin dynasties were the first important developmental period for traditional Chinese painting, marked by the appearance of paintings with true individuality. Scholar-bureaucrats of the time advocated free discussion and stressed the spirit while evaluating a person. Gu Kaizhi, a famous artist in the Eastern Jin Dynasty, was a representative of the spirit-oriented style. He insisted that the "spirit of a figure shall be expressed through outer appearances" and especially highlighted the traits of figures. While painting a Buddhist image for the Waguan Temple in Jiankang, Gu didn't draw the eyes until the rest of the painting was finished, which immediately made the image extremely vivid and won praise and adoration from all witnesses, who subsequently gave alms to the temple.

Frequent exchanges with ethnic groups in the Western Regions and foreign nations helped enrich the Chinese art forms, such as music, dance, and grotto sculptures in the Wei, Jin, Southern, and Northern dynasties. Grotto sculptures that combine sculpture and painting particularly reflect the highest achievements of the time. Yungang Grottoes in Pingcheng (present-day Datong, Shanxi), initiated in the early Northern Wei Dynasty, boast spectacular scale with more than 50,000 Buddhist statues and flying apsaras. The largest Buddhist statue among them, 13.7 meters high, was carved with superb craftsmanship. Affected by Indian Buddhist art styles, the Buddhist statues have high noses, deep-set eyes, and serious facial expressions, traits typical of the ethnic people of the Western Regions. Longmen Grottoes in Luoyang, Henan, were created after Emperor Wendi of the Northern Wei Dynasty moved the capital there. One-third of the thousands of grottoes and habitats were excavated during the Northern Wei Dynasty. The Buddhist statues, which look solemn and kindly, are dressed in exquisitely carved clothes, and show cultural features of the central plains.

The thoughts and culture of the Wei, Jin, and Southern and Northern dynasties were not interrupted in the era of confrontation between the Southern and Northern dynasties. On the contrary, they thrived and featured the dominance of the central plains culture and the fusion of diverse elements.

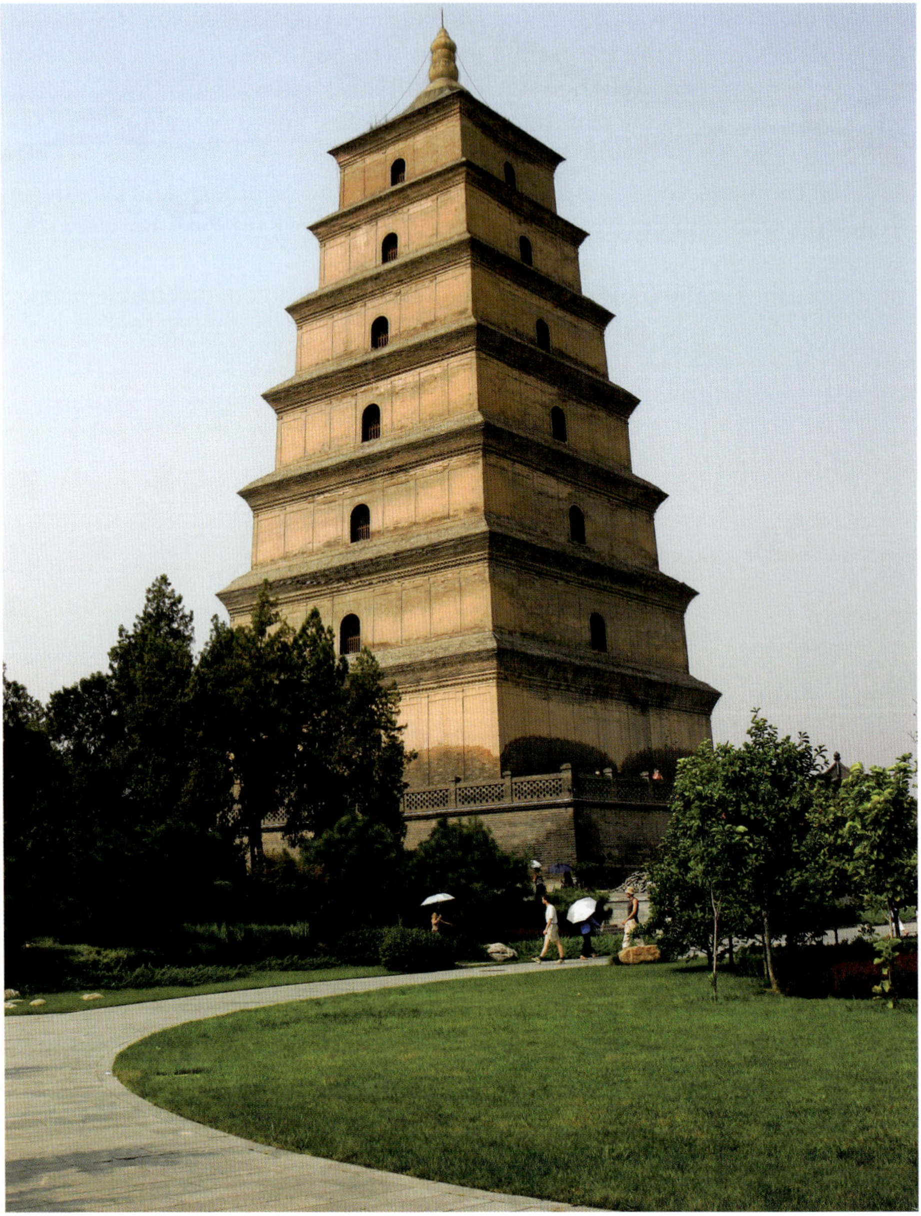

Chapter 6

The Sui and Tang Dynasties: A Prosperous and Open Age

Reunification and the Sui Dynasty

From the end of the 6th century to the early 10th century, a unified empire was rebuilt in China, and China entered into its heyday.

In 581, Yang Jian, a relative of the emperor of the Northern Zhou, replaced the dynasty and renamed the nation Sui, with its capital in Chang'an (today's Xi'an, Shaanxi). Yang Jian or Emperor Wendi of the Sui Dynasty was the son-in-law of a Xianbei noble and the granduncle of Emperor Jingdi of the Northern Zhou Dynasty, who succeeded to the throne at age seven. His family itself was the epitome of cultural fusion. Yang Jian was surrounded by a group of Han Chinese officials and Xianbei nobles deeply influenced by the Chinese culture. Furthermore, his position as a royal relative entrusted to assist handling politics rendered him great power and privileges. That facilitated the Sui's smooth replacement of Zhou and the subsequent establishment of the Sui Dynasty, the first dynasty ruled by the Han Chinese people and accepted by the minorities in the Northern Dynasties.

In 589, the Sui troops crossed the Yangtze River and ended the Chen Dynasty, capturing Jiankang within eight days and reuniting China after 400 years of separation. The Sui integrated the Yellow River and Yangtze River economic areas, greatly intensified the political, economic, and cultural ties between north and south, and promoted rapid growth of the economy.

After reunification, Emperor Wendi and his successor Emperor Yangdi promulgated a series of political and economic reforms to further intensify the centralized sovereignty and develop the economy. At the beginning of Emperor Yangdi's reign, he started to build Luoyang to better display its function as an economic center. Meanwhile, a 2000-km-long canal from Zhuojun (today's Tongzhou District, Beijing) in the north to Yuhang (today's Hangzhou, Zhejiang) in the south was also being built. The Grand Canal, linking five rivers—the Haihe, the Yellow, the Huaihe, the Yangtze, and the Qiantang rivers—became an important political, economic, and cultural tie, and played an important role in consolidating and promoting development along the canal.

The period from the start of the Sui Dynasty to the early regime of the Emperor Yangdi saw vast expanses of territory and powerful national strength. With substantial increases in population and land reclaimed, the state's official granaries could contain millions to thousands of millions of *dan* (one *dan* equals 50 kg). Extra granaries were built for relief in times of harvest failure. At the end of the regime of Emperor Wendi, "the grain storage nationwide could meet the needs of the people for the next 50 to 60 years."

During the reign of Emperor Yangdi, cloth and silk in Dongdu piled up like mountains. Stored products of the Sui Dynasty remained until the 20th year of the Tang Dynasty, inspiring Ma Duanlin, a historian of the Yuan Dynasty, to say "no other dynasty in history could compare with the Sui."

Emperor Yangdi determinedly and dauntlessly pursued his policy of reform, with great achievements. Most of his projects and political and economic reforms were of strategic significance, contributing to the flourishing

Gongchen Bridge in Hangzhou, the first bridge over the Grand Canal.

of the Tang Dynasty that followed. However, he paid little attention to the burden this put on the people. The emperor continuously engaged millions of people in civil works and engaged others in wars against (Korean) Koryo, resulting in desolated lands and starving people everywhere. Civilians went so far as to break their own hands and feet to escape from labor and army service. Emperor Yangdi's tyranny gave rise to nationwide peasant uprisings. Sui rapidly perished. In 618, Li Yuan seized the opportunity and established the Tang Dynasty in Chang'an.

Splendid Early Tang Dynasty

In 626, Li Shimin, honored with great feats in founding the Tang Dynasty and achieving national reunification, changed his reign title to Zhenguan. The powerful Sui Dynasty's quick collapse deeply shocked Li Shimin, Emperor Taizong of the Tang Dynasty. He realized emperors "will be the head when honest and upright, and isolated when brutal and tyrannical."

So, he successively freed 6,000 court girls and promised not to hold grand ceremonies of worship of heaven on mountains, pray for celestial beings, or conduct large-scale touring. He was also open to advice and tolerant toward his ministers' comments. His minister, Wei Zheng, often cited the end of the Sui Dynasty as a means to criticize his faults in public. Emperor Taizong, when extremely angered by the criticism, once told the empress that he would kill Wei Zheng sooner or later, but he eventually accepted Wei's suggestions. That gave rise to an open and free political atmosphere between the emperor and his ministers.

Emperor Taizong believed that "winning talented people is fundamental to national prosperity." With an open mind and unique insight, he didn't stick to the beaten track in employing talented people. He chose from former leaders of the insurgent troops, former ministers of the Sui Dynasty, favorite ministers of his political opponents, and ordinary people of humble birth. Those wise and brave people later played an important role in formulating and implementing reform and stabilizing the political situation.

Emperor Taizong of the Tang Dynasty.

During his reign, Emperor Taizong drew on the experiences and lessons of the Sui Dynasty, rolling out a series of policies aimed to stabilize society and develop the economy. He vigorously adjusted productive relations, social relations, and relations inside the ruling group, which resulted in clean politics and economic prosperity. The period was thus called the "Peaceful and Prosperous Zhenguan Period" in history.

Li Zhi, Emperor Gaozong, the successor of Emperor Taizong, was a coward and weak in health. Wu Zetian, the queen, was actively engaged in political affairs. After Li Zhi passed away, Wu Zetian ascended the throne in 690, becoming the only female emperor in Chinese history. She controlled the empire for half a century. Her father, a nouveau riche, rose with Li Yuan, Emperor Gaozu, but was looked down upon by the hereditary nobles for his humble origin. Emperor Gaozong's decision to install Wu Zetian as his empress was once strongly opposed by his senior ministers. However, with the support of those ministers with no scholarly background, Wu Zetian stepped onto the political stage as an empress. After seizing power, she ruled that all officials, including soldiers promoted to fifth-ranking officials due to their feats, should be included in the name catalog previously reserved exclusively for hereditary officials.

Wu Zetian, the only female emperor in Chinese history.

Chapter 6 The Sui and Tang Dynasties: A Prosperous and Open Age   **99**

A Kaiyuan Iron Ox from the Tang Dynasty at Pujindu. During the Kaiyuan Period, the Tang government cast 0.8 million kilograms of iron images of oxen, humans, mountains, and columns as ground anchors to build a pontoon bridge between the banks of the Yellow River at Pujindu. Salt, iron, and coal from Shanxi were subsequently transported across the Yellow River to Chang'an, Shaanxi Province.

She also put cruel officials in important positions so they could frame people for crimes and kill noted families and ministers who embraced resistance—as a way to break the tradition of prestigious families' monopoly of high rank and politics. Moreover, Wu held examinations and questioned applicants herself. She selected talents from common landlords regardless of rank or family. Luo Binwang, one of the four outstanding poets of the early Tang Dynasty, once wrote *A Call to Crusade* against Wu Zetian, saying she was ruthless and rapacious, and "is hated by both people and the god, and can't be tolerated by the heaven and earth." Instead of flying into a rage, Wu spoke highly of Luo's talent and chided the prime minister for not hiring him.

During her regime, Wu followed the policies of the Zhenguan Period: To reward farming and sericulture, and reduce labor service and taxation. Being prudent in wars resulted in continuous economic development. According to *Assembled Essentials of the Song Dynasty*, households nationwide rose from 3.8 million in 652 AD, a time right before she came into power, to 6.15 million in 705 AD, when she abdicated the crown.

In 712, Li Longji ascended the throne and was called Emperor Xuanzong. During his early term, he carried on reforms, adjusting official systems, and developing production. That led to a highly stable society, a thriving economy with bumper harvests and affordable grain, and a population growth of up to 10 million households. The period also saw an unprecedented development in handicrafts, such as porcelain and textiles, and a surge in iron product categories, scale of production, and new techniques. The state power of the Tang Dynasty had reached its culmination, and the period was thus honored as the Kaiyuan Flourishing Age.

Reforms of the Sui and Tang Dynasties

The prosperity of the early Tang hinged on the economic and social development then. Land cultivation and irrigation using bent shaft plows and scoop waterwheels granted greater freedom to individual peasants. This led to the rapid development of intensively cultivated small land parcels and produced a great number of middle and small landlords. Meanwhile, the population of decadent gentry and landlords, crushed by widespread peasant wars at the end of the Sui Dynasty, gradually declined. The individual cultivation-based landlords broke the fetters of hereditary noble households and started to play an important role in state politics, initiating a range of far-reaching innovations in the prevailing systems.

Establishment of the Three-Ministry and Six-Department System in the Sui and Tang dynasties represents a significant change in the ancient Chinese official system. *Zhongshu* Ministry (Imperial Secretariat), *Menxia* Ministry (Imperial Chancellery), and *Shangshu* Ministry (State) were the supreme administrative organizations of the country, in charge of decision-making and drafting orders, and the review and execution of state affairs, respectively. Under the Shangshu Ministry, six departments were set up. The Department of Civil Appointment was in charge of the appointment and assessment of officials. The Department of Finance was in charge of land resources, household registry, taxation, and financial affairs. The Department of Rites was in charge of ritual affairs, celebrations, sacrifices, schools, and imperial examinations. The Department of War was in charge of officer selection, serviceman registry, military orders, and weapons. The Department of Punishments was in charge of laws, orders, the judiciary, criminal punishment, and prisons. The Department of Works was in charge of civil engineering, irrigation and flood control, arable land, roads, and the like. The heads of these three ministries were prime ministers. They discussed state affairs and assisted the emperor in ruling the country, while supplementing each other and checking each other. The responsibilities of the six departments were well divided and became the formal administrative institutions of the country.

The expostulation system was designed to supervise and correct major policies of the court. Even orders of the emperors were examined in the Tang Dynasty. The Menxia Ministry had the exclusive right to reject reports of the officials and to review and return orders of the emperor. During the Zhenguan Period, the Wuhua Panshi system was also implemented, allowing officials of concerned departments to overview all major military events and present their views to the emperor for a final decision. To ensure administrative efficiency, officials who intentionally delayed the deadline of the joint signature would be punished.

The Wei, Jin, and Southern and Northern dynasties stressed family background when selecting officials. Descendants of noble birth could get promoted to ministers and monopolize the positions for generations, even though some were ignorant, incompetent, and unenterprising. But things had changed in the Sui and Tang dynasties with the increasingly bigger role of the

Civilian (left) and warrior figures (right) of the Tang Dynasty.

The Wild Goose Pagoda in Xi'an, built in the third year of the reign of Emperor Gaozong (652). The new *Jinshi* degree-holders of the imperial examinations of the Tang Dynasty carved their names on the pagoda tablets, considered a supreme honor for scholars.

emerging commoner-landlord class, hence the establishment of the official selection system with imperial examinations.

Under the imperial exam system, the central government chose officials via regular imperial examinations and emphasized that capabilities were the standard for official selection. The imperial examinations were divided into *Jinshi* and *Mingjing*. Mingjing was designed to test the capability of reciting classics. Jinshi mainly focused on poetry and ode writing and strategies on current affairs, aimed at testing the person's capability of governing political affairs and solving social problems. The scholars had to pass further examinations of the organization department. Outstanding ones would be chosen and appointed. Another way to be appointed was to first act as an assistant in the local government, and then be recommended by senior officials.

Chapter 6 The Sui and Tang Dynasties: A Prosperous and Open Age

Stone rubbing of *Jinshi* Scholars' names on Wild Goose Pagoda tablets.

The official selection system based on imperial examinations broke the monopoly of the rich and powerful families, expanded the social foundation for the central regime, and injected a fresh force into social development. It created a relatively objective, equitable, and fair official selection mechanism, ensuring the continuous introduction of talented people and providing the state organization with a systematic guarantee of vigorous, stable, and efficient performance.

Tang's laws simplified the system of the Sui and had lighter penalties. Execution was very prudently applied, and five reviews were required. *Comment on Law of the Tang Dynasty,* the earliest extant legal code in China, has had a great influence on Asian countries throughout history.

The Early Tang Dynasty made certain adjustments based on the System of Equal Distribution of Land adopted since the Northern Wei and Sui dynasties. Provisions on awarding land according to numbers of slaves, maids, *buqu* (a social class between slaves and ordinary people), and cattle were canceled, keeping the despotic economy in check to some extent. Officials of five-rank (out of nine) or higher and those honored due to military feats were also awarded a certain parcel of land based on rank and merit, which served as an important way to support the emerging landlord class. Restrictions on sales of some types of land, like permanently held land and bestowed land, were loosened, further facilitating the development of private ownership.

With regard to the tax and corvee system, the Tax-Labor-Substitution System was implemented widely, which allowed replacement of corvee with payment by silk or cloth. In the middle Tang Dynasty, land mergers and the false reporting of household population led to the collapse of the System of Equal

Farming, a fresco from Dunhuang.

Distribution of Land. The court also changed the Tax-Labor-Substitution System to the Dual-Tax System, speeding the process of land privatization and the development of the commoner-landlord economy. The Dual-Tax Law stipulated that taxes be levied on property size—not on population—which released control over peasants. In addition, coins largely replaced physical goods as a means of paying tax, and nobles, bureaucrats, and merchants were all required to pay tax, too. That expanded the government's tax base and increased its revenue.

These significant systematic reforms implemented in the Sui and Tang dynasties reflected the development of the emerging commoner-landlord system and their political pursuits as well. They initiated a new trend for future social development and made the Sui and Tang dynasties a critical turning point in ancient Chinese history.

Hu and Han are "Members of One Family"

The Tang Dynasty was witness to another grand unification. The central government and the border ethnic groups developed closer relations. Emperor Taizong announced that, "I love the Han and ethnic groups equally, though most have favored the former all along."

After defeating the Eastern Turks in the South Desert during the Zhenguan Period, the Tang Dynasty adopted the policy of "all tribes following their local customs." Turkish aristocrats were still the governors, and generals had jurisdiction over tribal members. All previous ethnic customs and ways of life were retained. In the meantime, nearly 10,000 Turks moved to Chang'an, including more than 100 Turkish chieftains who were honored as senior officials with five-rank or above. Before long, the Tang Dynasty set up the Protectorate General of Anxi in the Western Regions; the Protectorate General of Beiting was further established during the regime of Wu Zetian, respectively governing areas south and north of Tianshan Mountain.

Moved by the open policy, chieftains of northwestern tribes addressed Emperor Taizong respectfully as Tian Khan (the great heavenly Khan) and supported him as their mutual leader. During the later Zhenguan Period, more than ten tribes in the North Desert, including the Huihe, submitted to the Tang Dynasty in succession, and opened a "road of Khan" in the desert. The court set up sixty-eight posthouses along the path to receive emissaries and offer services for traveling businessmen. After that, Emperor Suzong, Emperor Dezong, and Emperor Muzong all married one of their princesses to the Huihe Khan for peace-making purposes.

Emperor Taizong also accepted the request of Songzan Gambo, the chieftain of Tubo on the Tibetan Plateau, to marry Princess Wencheng to him. When the princess entered Tibet, she brought handiworks, grains, vegetable seeds, herbal medicines and tea, as well as more than 100 kinds of production techniques and medical books, making Tubo "gradually affected by the advanced culture" and greatly boosting the local economic and cultural growth.

Emperor Taizong of the Tang Dynasty Meeting Tibetan Emissaries (part) by Yan Liben portrays Tibetan King Songzan Gambo's envoys to Chang'an, where he seeks a marriage alliance with the Tang Dynasty.

After succeeding to the throne, Emperor Gaozong conferred the title of Chief Commandant of Escorting Cavalry upon Songzan Gambo and honored him as the King of Xihai Jun. During the reign of Emperor Zhongzong, he further married Princess Jincheng to Chidai Zhudan, the king of Tubo, who called himself the "nephew" of the emperor, and said, "Tubo and Han are members of one family."

In 823, the Tang Dynasty and Tubo entered into an alliance in Changqing. The Monument to the Tang-Tubo Alliance still stands in front of the Jokhang Temple in Lhasa today, serving as witness to the friendly relations between the Tang Dynasty and Tibet.

The mid-seventh century saw the rise of Heishui and Sumo tribes of the Mohe ethnic group in the Songhua River and Heilongjiang River basins. During the Zhenguan Period, Heishui Mohe started to pay tribute to the Tang Dynasty. In the early eighth century, the Tang Dynasty established the Heishui Governor-General Mansion and appointed its chieftain as the governor. In the beginning of Kaiyuan Period, Emperor Xuanzong conferred the title of King of Bohai upon Dazuorong and honored him as the Governor of Huhan Prefecture. Bohai had close relations with the central plains, and its capital, Shangjing Longquanfu (present-day Bohai Town, Anning City, Heilongjiang Province) was modelled on Chang'an of the Tang Dynasty. The prefecture and county system were also copied, as well as the advanced production techniques of the central plains.

A Dunhuang fresco depicting the integration of Han and northern ethnic groups in music and dance during the Tang Dynasty.

There were six tribes—Six Zhaos—in the Erhai area during the Sui and Tang dynasties. In the early eighth century, the Tang Dynasty supported South Zhao to unify the Six Zhaos, and Emperor Xuanzong honored its chieftain as the King of Yunnan. The advanced techniques from the central plains promoted the development of the local economy. When growing stronger, South Zhao came into conflict with the Tang Dynasty, resulting in a time of alternating war and peace. At the end of the eighth century, South Zhao once again submitted to the Tang Dynasty. In 794, the King of South Zhao met the emissary team of the Tang Dynasty at the Divine Temple in Diancang Mountain. From then on, South Zhao has been deeply affected by the Tang Dynasty in a wide range of aspects, such as administrative organization, production techniques, and way of living, making great contributions to the development of the southwestern regions.

With more than 800 provinces, prefectures, and counties established in the border areas inhabited by ethnic groups, the early Tang Dynasty boasted a territory reaching the sea in the east, the Anxi and Congling Mountain areas in the west, the Mongol Plateau in the north, and the South Sea in the south, and was characterized by unprecedented affluence and power. Both folk customs and art also showed signs of communication and the merging of ethnic and Han cultures. The ethnic groups greatly appreciated silk and porcelain and central plains food, like dumplings, and tea became an important material for exchange.

Meanwhile, the central plains saw the popularity of ethnic clothes and food. Frescoes and sculptures from the Tang Dynasty also reflect the distinct glamour of the Western Regions, either in expression or artistic style. The dancers and bands were mostly from diverse ethnic groups, and the musical instruments include those of both ethnic and Han styles, manifesting the characteristics of a time when ethnic groups and Han were members of one family.

Openness and Communication

The Sui and Tang dynasties boasted developed inbound and outbound trade routes. The land route ran from present-day North Korea in the east, through the Silk Road, to present-day India, Pakistan, Afghanistan, Iran, and the Persian Gulf in the west. It further extended to many European and African countries through Central Asia and the Mediterranean Sea. The sea route started from today's South Korea and Japan in the east and ended in the Persian Gulf in the west. Tang Dynasty policies that encouraged openness and communication, as well as the smooth land and sea routes, gave rise to extremely frequent Sino-foreign exchanges.

Japan had sent its emissaries to the Tang Dynasty thirteen times, with hundreds of Japanese students going with each mission. In 645, Japan launched

Taika Reform, taking the Tang Dynasty as a model in many aspects including political, legal, and land and tax systems, and even the construction of its capital city. Ku Kai, a Japanese scholar monk who once went to the Tang Dynasty to study Buddhism, adopted the strokes of Chinese characters to create Japanese letters called Katakana.

Jianzhen, a monk of the Tang Dynasty, tried to cross the ocean eastward to Japan but failed multiple times. He finally did it on his sixth attempt, at the age of sixty-six. Jianzhen himself carried out monkhood initiation for the Japanese emperor, empress, and prince, as well as for ordinary people from various circles. He gave lectures on Buddhism and introduced Chinese medicine, architecture, sculpture, calligraphy, painting, and other knowledge to the Japanese people. In the late seventh century, Silla on the Korean Peninsula also sent groups of students to the Tang Dynasty, and imitated such Tang systems as the six departments and official selection through imperial examinations. Deeply affected by the Tang Dynasty, Silla displayed a strong Tang style in a wide range of areas from science and technology to art, literature, and folk customs.

Statute of Jianzhen.

Chapter 6　The Sui and Tang Dynasties: A Prosperous and Open Age　　**109**

Portrait of Xuanzang.

During the early Zhenguan Period, the senior monk Xuanzang made an arduous journey west to India, where he studied Buddhism earnestly for five years. Then he toured around many other counties to give Buddhist lectures. Seventeen years later, he returned to Chang'an, where he devoted himself to translating Buddhist sultras, and *The Buddhist Records of the Western Regions*, compiled by his disciples, describes what he saw and heard along his westward journey. He was also entrusted by Emperor Taizong to translate the *Tao Te Ching* into Sanskrit. Xuanzang's efforts with Buddhist scriptures promoted Sino-Indian cultural exchanges and had a great influence on Chinese history.

The Tang Dynasty opened itself to the outside world in an all-around way and carried out extensive communication with foreign countries, keeping commercial ties with more than seventy, including countries in West Asia, Europe,

Tang Dynasty Colored Pottery Figures. On the camel are performers from Middle Asia.

and Africa. The government permitted foreigners to live in China, marry Chinese people, and take part in Chinese examinations for official selection. Some foreigners even acted as military officials of the court or servants of the emperor. The city of Chang'an, capital of the Tang Dynasty, covered an area of 84 square kilometers and had a population of nearly one million, the world's largest international city then. Arabia saw the establishment of an Arab Empire that spanned across Asia, Africa, and Europe in the seventh century, but it collapsed in the ninth century. Europe was in the medieval era of division and chaos. The prosperous Sui and Tang dynasties, while imposing a far-reaching influence on neighboring countries and regions, extensively absorbed foreign cultures to enrich and develop the Chinese culture. Merchants, scholars, and people of ethnic groups, as well as foreign emissaries and students, gathered in

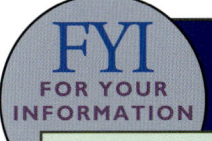

FYI — THE PROSPEROUS TANG DYNASTY IN THE EYES OF WESTERNERS

> The early Tang of China featured extreme courteousness, advanced culture, and far-reaching influence, presenting a sharp contrast to the corruption, chaos, and division of the western world.
>
> While western minds were obsessed with religion and kept in a state of darkness, Chinese minds were open, compatible, and curious.
>
> —H. G. Wells, *The Outline of History*

the capital city of Chang'an, and grand feasts filled with singing and dancing were widespread. Women also wore ethnic clothing, rode horses, played ball games, and joined various sorts of social, sports, and entertainment activities. The society was full of vigor and vitality.

Brilliant Culture of the Sui and Tang Dynasties

The Sui and Tang dynasties, integrated in territory, prosperous in economy, and liberal in politics, promoted the quick development of culture and education. A complete school education system from the central to the local was established, which taught law, mathematics, and other major subjects. The social reforms and systematic renovation during the period also gave fresh impetus to advances in science, technology, literature, and art.

The period saw two great inventions that had a significant impact upon human civilization, namely wood block printing and gunpowder.

Enlightened by the techniques of seal engraving and printing from engraved stones in ancient China, wood-block printing began in the early Tang Dynasty. The Zhenguan Period left records of engraving and printing. The *Vajra Sutra,* an exquisitely engraved printing work, done with bright ink in the ninth year of the Xiantong Period of the Tang Dynasty (868), is the earliest dated wood-block document in the world. The invention of wood-block printing that followed in the wake of paper making played a significant role in keeping, spreading, and developing human culture.

In the early Tang Dynasty, Taoists stumbled upon the formula for gunpowder as they were making medicines. Sun Simiao, a medicine expert

Vajra Sutra printed in the ninth year of Xiantong Period of Tang (868).

in the early Tang Dynasty, recorded how to make gunpowder in the book *Alchemical Scriptures*. "First, put two taels of sulphur and another two taels of saltpeter into an earthen pot, then burn the Chinese Honeylocust hot and put it inside the pot, which will jointly create raging flames." There are other records of peasant insurgent troops that used gunpowder in wars at

Zhaozhou Bridge in Hebei, built in the Sui Dynasty, is the earliest, well-preserved, single-arch stone bridge in the world.

Chapter 6 The Sui and Tang Dynasties: A Prosperous and Open Age

the end of the Tang Dynasty. In addition, gunpowder was used in hunting, excavation, and stone extraction.

Ancient Chinese architectural art entered a period of maturity during the Sui and Tang dynasties. Yu Wenkai, an architect of the Sui Dynasty, used drawings and models to design and direct the construction of the beautifully laid out city of Daxing, which was later expanded into Chang'an (Xi'an) during the Tang Dynasty. This and his design and construction of Luoyang demonstrate the era's superb techniques in urban construction. The Zhaozhou Bridge, designed and built by Li Chun, a workman of the Sui Dynasty, is a single-hole, stone arch bridge 37 meters wide and more than 50 meters long. Reputed as "a wonder in world bridge-building history," it is well preserved until today.

The Tang Dynasty was the golden age of ancient Chinese poetry, with more than 50,000 poems passed down to present. Prosperity, openness, cultural diversity, and the enterprising spirit encouraged by the fresh official selection system combined to inspire the brilliance of Tang poetry characterized by orderly rhythm and proper parallelism. Gao Shi, Cen Sen, Wang Changling, and other frontier poets sang the praises of soldiers and officers. Poems written by Meng Haoran, Wang Wei, and other idyllic poets expressed the peaceful harmony between man and nature.

The Drunk Li Bai, by Su Liupeng, depicts Li Bai supported by two eunuchs after getting drunk in the palace of Emperor Xuanzong.

The most notable poets in the Tang Dynasty were Li Bai and Du Fu. Li Bai, called the God of Poetry, wrote poems that are bold and unconstrained, representing the vigorous and personality-oriented spirit in the prosperous period of the Tang Dynasty.

Du Fu, called the Saint of Poetry, was destitute and homeless and worried about the country and the people throughout his life. His poems reflect social reality, especially people's difficult lives amid the chaos caused by war. His poems were heavy and indignant, and were called "poetic history."

Paintings of the Tang Dynasty featured greater scope of subject, with figures, landscapes, and flowers and birds becoming independent fine art forms. Systematic painting techniques were invented, and diverse schools of painting emerged. Wu Daozi, respected as the Saint of Artists, combined his interest in calligraphy with line drawing, achieving the artistic effect of "drifting clothes and moving lines."

The national reunification in the Sui and Tang dynasties brought about the combination of the southern and northern calligraphic styles—gracefulness and vigorousness. The styles of Ouyang Xun, Yan Zhenqing, and Liu Gongquan were representative of the times. Ouyang's scripts were bold and dignified. Yan's calligraphy was round and simple, while Liu had a serious and vigorous style. Zhang Xun and Huai Su were famous for cursive hand, which is smooth, drifting, and unrestrained.

Affected by foreign cultures, the music and dance of the Sui and Tang dynasties were colorful in style. Emperor Xuanzong, acquainted with music rhythms, once imparted dancing and singing techniques to 300 musicians in a pear park, and composed "Dancing in a Gauze Costume" by drawing on the styles of Western Regions.

Yan Qingli Stele by Yan Zhenqing in the Tang Dynasty.

Chapter 6 The Sui and Tang Dynasties: A Prosperous and Open Age 115

Ladies of Kingdom Guo on a Spring Outing (part) represents the life of the ladies in the Tang Dynasty.

Colored statue in Dunhuang Mogao Grottoes. The Bodhisattva, with a round face, plump stature, and coiled bun, loosely dressed in silk, reflects the prevailing aesthetics of the Tang Dynasty.

The Mogao Grottoes, located in Dunhuang, Gansu, a key site along the Silk Road, is the world's largest and best-preserved Buddhist artistic treasure. More than 3,000 colorful sculptures and 45,000 square meters of frescoes have been preserved at present, most of which are works dating from the Sui and Tang dynasties. Statues with different facial expressions look vivid and lively, and the frescoes' smooth, drifting lines are splendid and charming.

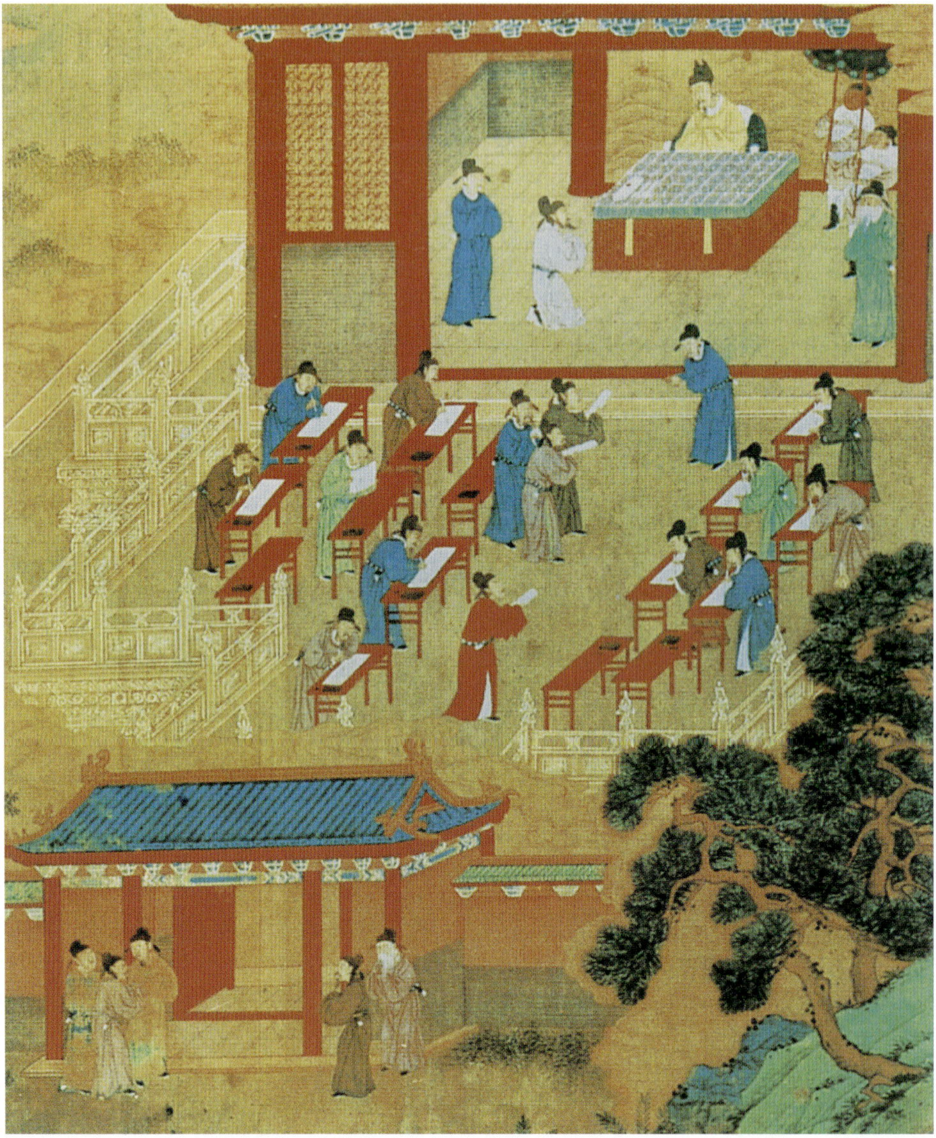

Chapter 7

The Song and Yuan Dynasties: Cultural Collision and Fusion and Socioeconomic Advances

Confrontations between the Northern and Southern Song Dynasties, and the Liao, Xixia, and Jin Dynasties

The later period of Emperor Xuanzong's reign was marked by political corruption and weakened power and control. Eunuchs seized power in the court, and warlords held control over local areas. The empire was rocked by sweeping peasant uprisings at the end of the Tang Dynasty and was put to an end by warlords in 907. In the next fifty years, the Yellow River Valley was under the reign of the Later Liang (907–923), the Later Tang (923–936), the Later Jin (936–947), the Later Han (947–950), and the Later Zhou (951–960), collectively called the Five Dynasties. The period from 960 to 1368 saw three historical stages: the Northern Song confronting the Liao and the Xixia, the Southern Song confronting the Jin, and unification by the Yuan Dynasty.

In 960, General Zhao Kuangyin initiated a mutiny and overturned the Later Zhou to establish the Song Dynasty in Bianjing (today's Kaifeng, Henan), called the Northern Song period. The Northern

Zhao Kuangyin, Emperor Taizu of the Song Dynasty.

Song successfully quelled the various rebellions and reunited the central plains and spacious southern areas.

Having learned what happened when key ministers usurped power and warlords revolted, the Northern Song applied a series of measures to "deprive them of their power, control their finance and grain, and reorganize their forces."

In the central government, the prime minister's power was divided into three independent sections to enhance the emperor's control. *Tongpan* (magistrates) were established in local counties to supervise local governors. On the military front, the right to lead and the right to dispatch were separated. The imperial guard troop was regularly changed, but the leader did not shift with the troop. The central government also selected the elite of local troops to enter the imperial guard troop to defend the capital and weaken local units.

All tax income was submitted to the central government except a small percentage for local expenses. These measures to reinforce central power and control were helpful in maintaining unity and stability and promoting economic development. However, some over-corrective actions resulted in redundancies, low efficiency, enormous expenditure, underperforming military direction, poor effectiveness in battle, and other negative effects.

In 916, the Khitan chieftain Yelü Abaoji, who lived in the desert and northeastern regions, came to the throne and built the Liao regime in Shangjing (today's Lindong Town, Balin Left Banner, Inner Mongolia). The Khitans, who mainly lived as nomads, fishing and hunting, gradually learned farming and settlement-building, and invented characters based on Chinese character components. The Khitan nobles constantly looted southward and forced the Later Jin to cede Youzhou, Jizhou, and fourteen other prefectures, then occupied the North China Plain.

In 1004, about 200,000 Liao soldiers attacked the Northern Song and approached Tanzhou from the north side of the Yellow River near the capital, Bianjing. Prime Minister Kou Zhun advised Emperor Zhenzong to lead the army himself. The Emperor-led Song army had high morale and defeated the Liao troops. Emperor Zhenzong accepted the peace negotiation under an advantageous condition and signed the Chanyuan Agreement. Under the agreement, the Song would give Liao 100,000 taels of silver and 200,000 bolts of thin silk each year, the Liao would withdraw their army to the boundary, and both parties would become brother countries. Although the Chanyuan Agreement, a product of the balance of power of Song and Liao, further increased the Northern Song people's burden, a roughly century-long peace was achieved after the agreement. Both parties continued to trade, resulting in a flourishing economy and cultural development.

In the early Northern Song Dynasty, the nomadic Dangxiang ethnic group gradually sprang up in the northwestern region. In 1038, Dangxiang Chieftain Yuanhao of the Xixia ascended the throne in Xingqing (today's Yinchuan, Ningxia). The Xixia often invaded the Northern Song and frequently won. However, the battles destroyed their normal mutual trade. The Northern Song's firm defense caused grain shortages and the financial collapse of the Xixia. In 1044, Yuanhao offered a peace agreement to the Northern Song. Both parties agreed that Yuanhao would cancel the title of emperor and submit to the Northern Song. The Northern Song gave silver, silk, and tea to Xixia as "annual payment" and reopened border trade. From then on, Song and Xia maintained a generally peaceful trade relationship.

In the middle and later Northern Song Dynasty, the Jurchen ethnic group that fished and hunted in the Heilongjiang River Valley steadily rose up in arms against the oppression of the Liao. In 1115, the Wanyan Tribe's Chieftain Aguda came to the throne and set up the Jin regime in Huining (today's A'cheng in Heilongjiang). After exterminating the Liao in 1125, Jin initiated an invasive war against the Northern Song and captured Bianjing the next year. In 1127, Emperors Huizong and Qinzong were captured, marking the end of the Northern Song.

In 1127, Zhao Gao ascended to the throne and relocated the capital to Lin'an (today's Hangzhou, Zhejiang), known as the Southern Song. Under the leadership of Yue Fei and other famous generals, the military and civilian forces of the Southern Song bravely fought against invasion by the Jin troops and won major victories. But, vilified by those officials advocating surrender, Yue Fei was executed by Emperor Gaozong Zhao Gou under a fabricated charge. In 1141, the Song and Jin inked an agreement, stating that the Southern Song emperor would submit to the Jin, cede the region north of the Huaihe River, and pay silver and silk as annual tributes to the Jin.

Four Generals Resisting the Jurchens, featuring Liu Guangshi, Han Shizhong, Zhang Jun, and Yue Fei of the Southern Song Dynasty.

Pursuant to this agreement, the Southern Song occupied a mere corner on the southern bank of the Yangtze River, a result of the Song–Jin confrontation in the south and north, respectively.

The northern ethnic groups absorbed the culture of the central plains during their expansion. The Liao, Xixia, and Jin dynasties successively imitated the political system of the central plain dynasties, rewarded land reclamation, and moved Han people northward, resulting in further economic exchange and ethnic amalgamation.

In 947, Liao Dynasty troops captured Kaifeng and met with strong opposition on their way back to the north after plundering local properties. Emperor Taizong of the Liao Dynasty drew two major lessons from the war—the futility of "indulging troops in plundering the city" and "robbing people of their private properties." He further shifted his policies to "governing areas based on local customs" and implemented the policy of "dividing officials into two parts, with one part governing the Khitans based on the state systems and the other governing the Han Chinese people based on the Han systems." In the regime of Emperor Shengzong, the two different systems adopted in the north and south were gradually integrated into one, with the Han Chinese system widely applied in the central plains. Encouraged by such measures as awarding farm cattle to the poor and exempting those that reclaimed barren land from tax and duties, the vast expanses of the northern border areas were developed during this period.

In the middle of the 10th century, Liaohai in northeastern China saw a thriving phenomenon described as "hundreds of thousands of registered households and "thousands of miles of reclaimed fields." Meanwhile, great advances were taking place in iron-smelting, silk-weaving, porcelain-making, wood block printing, and other handicraft sectors.

The Xixia in northwestern China implemented two systems, namely the Han Chinese system and the Dangxiang system, for its official positions, and imitated the official selection process via imperial examinations. The rulers of Xixia attached great importance to the culture of the central plains. Xixia characters were based on Han characters, classic books of the central plains were translated and printed by movable type printing techniques, and coins with the Chinese characters "Tian Shou Tong Bao" were cast. With regard to production, Xixia's handicraft sectors, such as iron-smelting, printing, porcelain, and wool textiles, were in leading positions. Printing works with Xixia characters that have been preserved until today are the world's earliest known movable type printing work. With advanced vertical bellows, Xixia ironworks could produce extremely sharp weapons, reputed as the "No. 1 in the world." With regard to agriculture, the farming techniques of the central plains were adopted in an all-around way, and irrigation systems were built in river bends and in

Chapter 7 The Song and Yuan Dynasties   **123**

Liao Dynasty attendants and horses in a procession.

Iron Smelting in Xixia.

the Hexi Corridor areas, making great contributions to the development of the northeastern regions.

After eliminating the Liao and Northern Song dynasties and occupied areas north of the Huaihe River, the Jin Dynasty implemented a series of reforms in order to better manage the highly developed farming areas. Wanyan Liang, King Hailing of the Jin Dynasty, who was familiar with Chinese characters and loved reading Chinese books, often discussed political affairs with Confucian scholars. In 1153, he moved the capital from Shangjing Huining (present-day Harbin) to Yanjing (present-day Beijing), a city with vast expanses of fertile land, full of energetic and civilized citizens. By imitating the Liao and Northern Song dynasties, the king implemented all-around reforms of official systems in 1156, which restricted the hereditary privileges of the Jurchen nobles and established a new regime characterized by centralized administration.

The Jin also encouraged the Jurchens to move southward to the central plains, promoting their move into the land tenancy system. The Jin Dynasty also printed money and molded cooper and silver coins to advance handicrafts and commerce. Meanwhile, the Jurchens were encouraged to marry the Han Chinese people. According to the *History of Jin,* during the two

The Marco Polo Bridge (Lugou Bridge), built after Jin's capital relocation to Zhongdu (Beijing), is 266.5 meters long. Sitting on its rails are 501 large and small carved stone lions.

decades following the capital move, the Jurchens gradually changed their former customs and practiced those of Han people in daily life, in music, and in many other aspects. Even the descendants of royal families "had practiced Han customs since their childhood" as they knew little about their own Jurchen culture.

Through decades of confrontation, collision, and communication, the ethnic groups and cultures of north and south further blended on the basis of the culture of the central plains.

Social Reforms and the Highly Developed Civilization of the Song Dynasty

By implementing a series of measures designed to intensify their centralized regimes, the Northern and Southern Song dynasties ended the divisions caused by the Five Dynasties after the Tang Dynasty, and moved forward to achieve reunification and stability. In the meantime, troops and people in the central plains bravely fought against attacks from northern nomadic ethnic groups, offering a relatively peaceful environment for the southern areas that saw fast social and economic growth.

The Song Dynasty carried on the reforms of the Sui and Tang, pushing forward profound changes in society. The Song "didn't curb land mergers" and allowed the free sale of land. In the mid-Northern Song Dynasty, most land was privately owned by middle and small landlords. Agriculture and handicraft sectors saw the emergence of contractual relationships. Tenant peasants and craftsmen were formally registered by the state.

Porcelain Pillow for Child. The porcelain industry of the Song Dynasty thrived, and a great deal of porcelain ware, silk, and tea was marketed all over the world via sea routes.

The land tenancy system and yeoman economy formed the mainstay of the national economy, and private handicraft workshops enjoyed rapid growth. In 1027, Emperor Renzong explicitly ordered that tenant peasants should move freely after tenancy contracts ended, and that landowners couldn't arbitrarily block their way. Later on, it was further stipulated that landlords couldn't use the tenant peasants' families as servants, and that when a tenant peasant died, "his wife who gets remarried is allowed to do so and his daughter can marry anybody she likes."

Most handicraft workshops also employed craftsmen, paying wages based on contracts, leaving craftsmen relatively free.

The adoption of land tenancy and employment systems were landmark reforms that resulted in high enthusiasm among the working people and greatly boosted social and economic growth.

The population at the end of the Northern Song Dynasty increased to 100 million, providing vast numbers of people for the workforce. Large-scale reclamation of terraces and low-lying fields resulted in more farmland—twice the area before. New types of farm equipment, such as plowshares with steel blades and seedling horses for paddy rice planting, were widely used for intensive farming. Champa paddy rice, a superior breed from Vietnam, was introduced and popularized, greatly increasing grain output. In the Southern Song Dynasty, the proverb —"When the area around Dongting Lake has a good harvest, the entire country has enough food"—spread across the country, showing that the national economic center had shifted from the Yellow River basin to the Yangtze River basin.

The Song Dynasty saw huge progress in its handicraft sector and boasted the largest coal yield in the world. The 500-meter laneway of one coal mine in Hebi, Henan, could accommodate hundreds of miners. Dating to the late Northern Song Dynasty, its facilities for lighting, ventilation, drainage, and mining techniques were close to modern levels. The production of smelted metals such as iron and copper reached the highest level in the world at the time, in both quality and quantity. During the reign of Emperor Shenzong of the Northern Song Dynasty, up to 100,000 copper-smelting craftsmen worked around Qianshan, Xinzhou, alone. The iron output of the Song Dynasty, roughly estimated, equaled the combined output of all the European countries in the 18th century. At the end of the Southern Song Dynasty, coke was used in iron smelting.

As for the textile sector, cotton-spinning production rose during the Southern Song Dynasty, with the appearance of new types of tools, such as spinning wheels, catapults, and weaving machines. Silk weaving was characterized by more colorful patterns and more diversified categories. The black and white porcelains produced in Jingdezhen, Jiangxi, were sold both at home and abroad, and led to the source of the word China, which literally means "the country of porcelains."

The Song Dynasty boasted an unprecedented prosperous commodity economy. Commercial activities went beyond the restrictions imposed during the Tang Dynasty, such as designated places and times for transactions. A large number of commodity distribution centers emerged around cities and major traffic routes in rural areas, leading to the formation of bazaars and towns of different sizes. In the Northern Song Dynasty, a commercial tax was levied in towns under the county level, resulting in dense commercial tax networks that made the tax a major source of government revenue.

In the early 11th century, Sichuan saw the presence of the world's earliest paper currency, *Jiaozi,* which was designed to facilitate commercial transactions. In the Southern Song Dynasty, *Huizi* and other types of paper currencies were widely circulated. Credit transactions with written deadlines and pledged by the rich emerged, as did other commercial means of payment, such as *Zhiku* for mortgages, *Didian* for storage and negotiation, and *Bianqianwu,* an officially-operated financial organization for exchange.

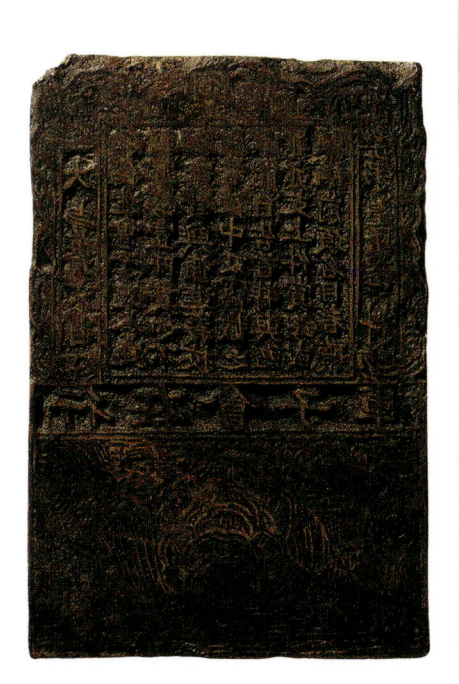

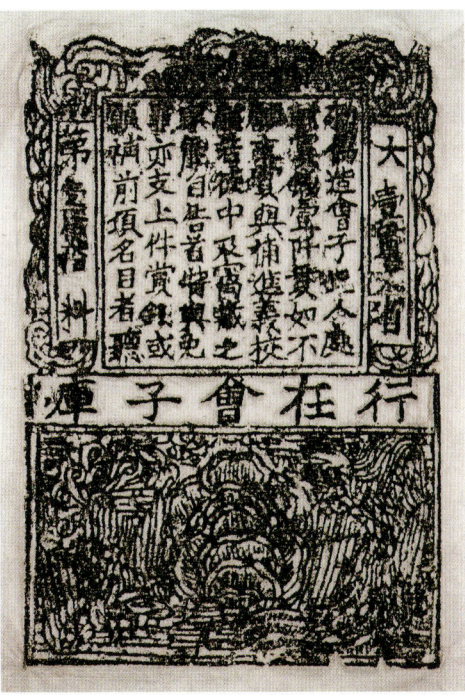

Wood block and print of *Huizi,* a paper currency of the Southern Song Dynasty.

A needle shop in Ji'nan, Shandong, designed its signpost like this: on the upper side was its name, "Ji'nan Liujia Needle Shop." In the middle stood a white rabbit accompanied by the words "recognizing the white rabbit in front of the shop as the symbol" down both sides. On the lower part was the advertisement: "needles made of superior steel bars are thin and easy to use. Anyone who buys the needles in large quantities for wholesale will enjoy special offers" —proof of the presence of trademarks and advertisements in the Song Dynasty, and the formation of a business mode that combined raw material procurement, processing, and wholesale trade.

Signpost of the Ji'nan Liujia Needle Shop.

According to historical records, the "transactions of gold, silver, and silk" in Bianjing of the Northern Song Dynasty took place in a lane in the southern part, where "buildings were spectacular and shops were spacious," and "every deal involved an amazing sum of money"—clearly resembling today's financial streets. The city of Bianjing saw densely-distributed shops in more than 400 sectors, including jewelry shops and high-grade gold and silver shops, and large markets for rice, vegetables, meat, fish, fruit, cloth, scarves, folding fans, belts, combs, needles, and ironware. Morning and night fairs operated along the streets.

The Song Dynasty also boasted an extremely advanced ship-making sector and ocean navigation techniques. Large ships capable of carrying tens of thousands of *dan* of grains were equipped with sealed cofferdams and drew deep with their pointed bottoms. Compasses were adopted for navigation, making trips both safe and speedy. Encouraged by the government, foreign trade developed quickly. Trading ships traveled to the West Pacific Ocean, Indian Ocean, and Persian Gulf, maintaining trade links with more than fifty countries and regions.

In addition, superintendents of merchant shipping were posted at important ports for administration. Special residential areas were built up for foreign merchants. Foreign markets and foreign language schools were also allowed. Arabian merchants were permitted to build mosques and public cemeteries. In the Southern Song Dynasty, Quanzhou became the world's largest international trade port. The combined foreign trade tax collected by the superintendents of merchant shipping in Quanzhou and Guangzhou

Imperial examinations in the Song Dynasty.

came to as much as 2,000,000 strings of copper coins, making up a big part of the government's revenue.

With the surge in economic development and social progress, social structure and social life in the Song Dynasty experienced profound changes. The Song Dynasty saw the final withdrawal of scholar-bureaucrats from the historical stage. Commoner-landlords who became officials through imperial examinations took major positions and constituted the backbone of the royal ruling group, which resulted in a free and rational political atmosphere.

According to historical records, Emperor Shenzong of the Song Dynasty once wanted to kill an official guilty of a crime, but was stopped by his ministers by citing the "domestic disciplines." The emperor then changed his mind and decided to send the official into exile, to which the ministers responded by saying, "it is better to die when living is a disgrace." Emperor Shenzong sighed, saying, "It's hard to do even one thing that could make

Along the River During the Qingming Festival, by Zhang Zeduan, vividly depicts the prosperity of Bianjing, capital of the Northern Song.

him feel good." The ministers said, "He might as well not do such kind of pleasant things."

From the Tang and Song dynasties forward, the country implemented a policy of sharing profits between government and business. With this policy, the troublesome operation of government-run businesses and franchises was contracted to businessmen, and part of the franchised business profits were shared. There were franchise certificates for government-monopolized products, such as salt and tea.

The participation of the businessmen improved efficiency and total profit. The actual income of the government from its share of franchised product revenues greatly increased. Many businessmen, especially those dealing in salt, cooperated with the government and got wealthy while serving the country, enjoying a respectable position. The Song Dynasty removed the restrictions that prevented descendants of those engaged in industrial and commercial business from being promoted to official status. Some rich businessmen married into royal families and those of court officials. Every time the results of the imperial examination for officials were released, the rich would hurry to select the successful candidates to be their sons-in-law, called "catching sons-in-law upon release of the candidates list."

The yeomen and semi-yeomen of the Song Dynasty accounted for more than 50 percent of the total population, tenant peasants 35 percent. Both tenant peasants and craftsmen held the status of civilians.

Economic growth and the rise of cities in the Song Dynasty led to an increase in the urban population. Non-peasant urban residents constituted the citizen class, which was dominated by businessmen, scholars, and intellectuals of the upper class, craftsmen in various fields, as well as mountebanks, fortune-tellers, street artists, and coolies. In the city of Bianjing, as depicted in *Along the River During the Qingming Festival,* a well-known painting of the Song Dynasty, the people are from all walks of life—carpenters, blacksmiths, silversmiths, pottery makers, barrel makers, painters, grass shoe weavers, fan makers, and mirror makers, as well as those selling oil, salt, paper, porridge, cakes, spices, and drugs. Jostling each other in the crowd and working hard for their own businesses, they present a vivid and energetic picture of urban life.

An overwhelming majority of the population in the Song Dynasty lived in rural areas. Most villagers could maintain their daily life and enjoyed a better life than before. They watched opera, listened to story-tellers, and had fun during their leisure time, greatly enriching their lives.

A thriving commodity economy and the growth of the citizen class gave rise to a booming citizen culture. Restaurants, hotels, and teahouses were widespread, the larger ones boasting a daily guest number of up to 1,000.

> # FYI
> FOR YOUR INFORMATION
>
> ## THE HIGHLY DEVELOPED CHINESE CIVILIZATION DURING THE SONG DYNASTY
>
> The Song Dynasty of China was so modern it surprised the whole world with its unique currency economy, paper notes, circulation bills, and highly developed tea and salt workshops. In areas of daily life, including art, entertainment, system, and craftsmanship, China was a country "second to none" in the world and was proud enough to categorize the rest of the world as "unenlightened regions."
>
> — Jacques Gernet, *Daily Life in China on the Eve of the Mongol Invasion, 1250-1276*

Recreational places in the cities, called "washe," hosted operas, acrobatics, history-telling, story-telling, sword-dancing, and other popular programs all night long, making it hard for passersby and spectators to tear themselves away. These thriving recreational places best demonstrate the tastes of the citizens and the vitality of ordinary life at that time.

The profound changes in the production relations and social structure during the Song Dynasty took social civilization to a higher level. Meanwhile, many fresh concepts emerged, a sign of an evolving trend toward modern society.

Yuan Empire Expanded the Unified Multi-ethnic Country

At the end of the 12th century, the Mongol ethnic group, previously under the rule of the Liao and Jin dynasties, grew stronger. In 1206, Temujin unified the Mongolian Plateau and established the state of Mongolia. He took the title of Genghis Khan. Expeditions led by him and his successors led to a rapid conquering of vast areas across Eurasia, bringing severe tribulations to the people.

While the Mongolian Empire straddled Europe and Asia, it was actually an unstable political and military union that lacked a common economic base and comprehensive laws and codes. In 1271, Kublai Khan changed the dynastic title to Yuan and set up the capital in Yanjing in order to move the sovereign center toward the central plains. In 1276, Yuan Dynasty troops captured Lin'an, announcing the end of the Southern Song. In 1279, Yuan unified the whole country.

Kublai, Emperor Shizu of the Yuan Dynasty, was entrusted to rule over the Han settlements in the South Desert in his early years, where he was deeply affected by the culture of the central plains. After ascending the throne, Kublai issued orders that "the state shall put its people first; people shall put food and clothes first; and food and clothes shall rely on agriculture and sericulture." He also opposed massacring the inhabitants of a captured city or making them servants, and forbade Mongolian nobles to arbitrarily take peasants' land and barren farming land to use as pastures. That way, the "bustling city wasn't affected by the war and remained as prosperous as before" when the troops of Yuan attacked Lin'an, the capital of the Southern Song Dynasty.

The policy of "attaching great importance to agriculture and sericulture" marked a significant turning point in the national policies of the Mongolian Empire, accelerating the transformation of a nomadic economy into a farming civilization. The court successively set up organizations and legal systems, and attached great importance to the popularization of advanced science and technologies, which proved fruitful. The Department of Agriculture was set up at the central level to take charge of nationwide agricultural and sericultural

Genghis Khan's Mausoleum.

affairs. Such criteria as "growing households," "increasing reclaimed fields," and "affordable tax and duties" were adopted as benchmarks of performance appraisal.

Many local governments commissioned paintings of farming and weaving, making "their officials acquainted with basic knowledge when they passed by the pictures." Encouraging and keeping a sharp focus on farming then became the fashion of the time. Kublai further ordered the Department of Agriculture to compile the *Essentials of Agriculture and Sericulture,* based on agricultural books of past and present. The book was circulated nationwide and some 10,000 copies were printed in 1332.

While abolishing some backward Mongolian systems like "integration of army and civilians," "dividing and sharing land among people," and hereditary official positions at prefecture and county levels, Kublai imitated the systems of former Tang, Song, Liao, and Jin dynasties, "establishing officials in charge of different affairs" to stabilize political situations and appease the public.

He established three major systems, namely *Zhongxingsheng* (administration), *Shumiyuan* (military affairs), and *Yushitai* (supervisory body), at the central level, and *Xuanzhengyuan* was set up to manage religious affairs and Tibet. In addition, *Xingsheng* was established as the local branch of the Zhongxingsheng, which was administrated by officials directly dispatched by the central government. In some remote areas inhabited by ethnic groups, *Xuanweisi* was set up for administration. To timely convey political orders and strengthen rule over local areas, *Tongzhengyuan* and

Kublai Khan, Emperor Shizu of the Yuan Dynasty.

posthouse systems were established nationwide, delivering top-to-bottom and bottom-to-top files and documents and offering traveling emissaries and officials daily necessities and traffic tools. All played a big role in consolidating the reunification.

To maintain the privileges of Mongolian nobles, the Yuan Dynasty classified people of different ethnic groups into four categories, namely Mongolians, Semu people, Han people, and South people, a sign of the dynasty's racial discrimination. On the other hand, the reunification of the Yuan Dynasty facilitated communication and exchange among people from all ethnic groups, resulting in the gradual amalgamation of the Khitan and Jurchen people, who moved southward to the central plains. Many Persian and Arabian Muslims immigrated to China and mixed with the Han and Mongolian people, shaping a new community known as the Hui ethnic group.

The Yuan Dynasty accomplished a much wider unification based on the civilization of the central plains. With vast territories, the empire expanded from areas north of the Yinshan Mountain in the north, to islands in South China Sea in the south, and stretched from present-day Sakhalin Island in the northeast to areas including Xinjiang and Central Asia in the northwest. Yuan officially included Tibet in the Chinese reign, and set up an executive secretariat in Yunnan and a patrol inspection administration in Penghu under the jurisdiction of Jinjiang County, Fujian, to administrate Penghu and Liuqiu (present-day Taiwan). The effort intensified Yuan's jurisdiction over and exploration in these areas. The Semu people, including the ethnic groups in Xinjiang, became part of the top ruling class of the Yuan Dynasty, increasing contact between the central plains and Xinjiang areas.

Following the historical retrogression caused by the dynastic change, the Yuan Dynasty witnessed rapid economic recovery and further consolidation of the unified multi-ethnic country. The period also saw smooth domestic and inbound–outbound traffic via both land and sea routes, as well as frequent Sino-foreign exchanges. Such cities as Dadu (present-day Beijing), Hangzhou, and Quanzhou were much more prosperous than in previous eras. Rabban Sawma, a Turkic monk, was once sent to Europe from Dadu. He established ties with the Roman Church and wrote what he saw and heard in Europe, the first Chinese records of this nature.

Marco Polo, an Italian businessman, arrived in Dadu in 1275 through the Silk Road and stayed in China for seventeen years, where he was once appointed by Kublai as an official of the Yuan Dynasty. His book, *The Travels of Marco Polo*, described many aspects of Chinese life, its bustling cities, social situations, folk customs, religious beliefs, and unique products, creating a sensation in European society.

Diversified Cultures in the Song and Yuan Dynasties

In the Song Dynasty, the previous monopoly of power by military officials was broken, and the national policy of "desisting from military activities and encouraging culture and education" was implemented. Against the backdrop of a thriving economy, the rise of the citizen class, and a relatively free political atmosphere, such fields as science and technology and ideology and culture took on a new look.

The period saw a complete education system with schools at different levels. Its institutes of higher learning included private academies besides *Guozijian* (the Imperial College) and *Taixue* (the highest seat of learning).

In 1308, Emperor Renzong of the Song Dynasty issued the order to establish schools in prefectures and counties nationwide. Meanwhile, private primary educational institutes and enlightening academies were widespread in both urban and rural areas. That elementary textbooks, such as *The Chinese Family Names* and *The Thousand-Character Classic,* were popularized in rural places, resulting in far higher levels of overall education and literacy than in any previous dynasty.

The scientific and technological achievements during the Song and Yuan dynasties were mainly reflected in the improvement in and wider application of printing techniques, the use of the compass and gunpowder, and the renovation in cotton-spinning techniques.

Bi Sheng, a commoner of the Northern Song Dynasty, invented movable type printing, the earliest of its kind in the world. The clay blocks he used could be disassembled and stored after typesetting and printing, and could be reused. The state of Xixia had movable wood type. Movable type printing was successively introduced into Korea, Japan, and the Arabian countries. The technique was further disseminated to Europe in the 13th century, and to Persia and Egypt through Xinjiang, thereby making a great contribution to world civilization.

The Song Dynasty saw extensive use of the compass in ocean navigation. Sailors fixed the magnetized steel needle on a compass with a carved-in mark to indicate north, making all-time navigation possible. In the Southern Song Dynasty, the compass was introduced to Europe through Arabia, laying a significant foundation for their global voyages and the discovery of the "New Continent."

Gunpowder-making techniques were improved, and gunpowder was widely used in military wars. In the Northern Song Dynasty, Guangbei Gongchengzuo, a state-owned arm shop, successively invented combustible and explosive

Chapter 7 The Song and Yuan Dynasties 137

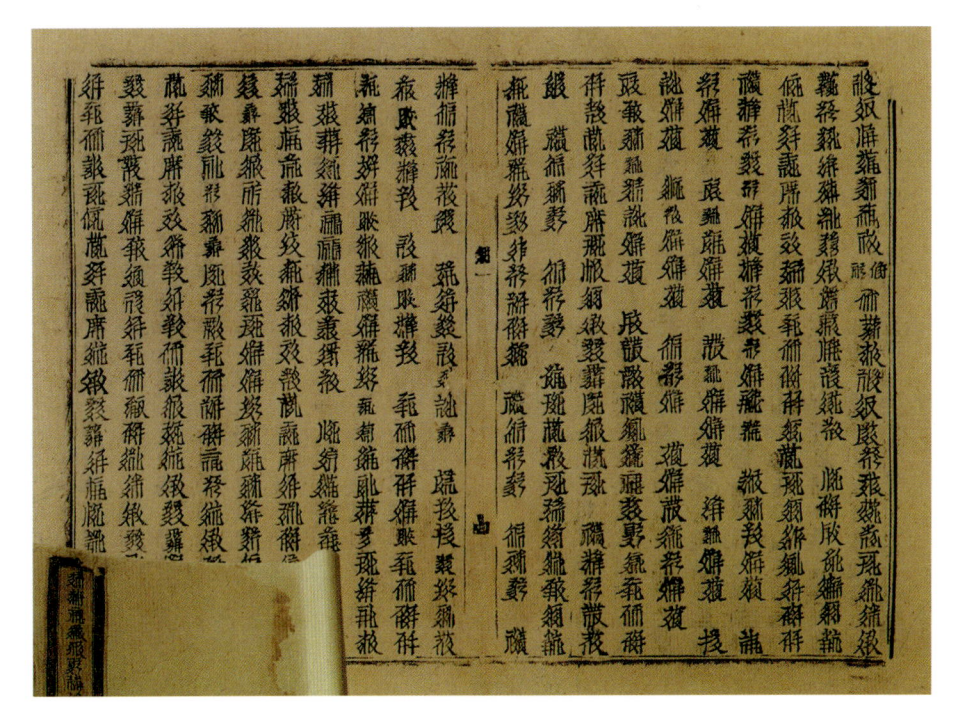

The sutra in Xixia characters, printed with movable type.

Copper gun of the Yuan Dynasty inscribed with "the third year of the Zhishun Period," indicating it was made in 1332. To date, it is the world's earliest preserved metal gun.

> ## THE GLOBAL IMPACT OF ANCIENT CHINA'S FOUR GREAT INVENTIONS
>
> The introduction and spread of China's four great inventions in the early European Renaissance period played a big role in the formation of the modern world. Papermaking and printing techniques were key factors in state reform and opened the door to public education. The invention of gunpowder helped end the feudal system and enhanced the national military force. The invention of the compass led to the discovery of America, making the entire world rather than Europe the stage for history.
>
> —Thomas Francis Carter, *The Invention of Printing in China and its Spread Westward*

firearms, as well as "toxic smoke balls" and pipe-shaped guns used to shoot bullets. In the middle 13th century, gunpowder was introduced to Arabian countries and later to Europe, arousing a sensation in European society.

While talking about Europe prior to the presence of textile machines in the 18th century, in his book *Das Capital,* Marx said, "It isn't easier to find a spinner who can spin two threads simultaneously than to find a double-headed man."

The cotton spinning wheel, an illustration from *The Book of Agriculture* by Wang Zhen of the Yuan Dynasty.

Philosopher Zhu Xi.

But in the early 14th century, Huang Daopo, a working woman in the Yuan Dynasty, could spin three threads at the same time. Based on the principle of how a hemp spinner worked, she restructured the one-thread spinner powered by hand into a three-thread spinner powered by feet. Huang further created a set of systematic advanced techniques used in every aspect of textile-making, from cottonseed grinding to cotton fluffing and spinning, to crossing threads and color matching in cloth weaving, which led to fundamental changes in the cotton textile sector in the Songjiang area, enabling it to become an important part of the handicraft industry. In the Yuan Dynasty, cotton gradually replaced silk and hemp, becoming a widely adopted raw material for clothes.

Guo Shoujing, an astronomer in the Yuan Dynasty, invented a new type of armillary sphere, an equatorial torquetum, which was compact and easy to use. It was created 300 years earlier than similar devices were invented in Europe. *Brush Talks from the Dream Brook,* written by Shen Kuo of the Northern Song Dynasty, covers the latest achievements in a wide range of fields, including astronomy, geography, mathematics, chemistry, and medical science. It was "a milestone in the Chinese history of science."

Chinese philosophy underwent great changes in the Song Dynasty. Cheng Hao and Cheng Yi of the Northern Song Dynasty and Zhu Xi of the Southern Song Dynasty abstracted the concepts of the three cardinal guides and five ethical norms of "law," and set up the Neo-Confucianism, also known as "Cheng-Zhu Neo-Confucianism." From the height of philosophy they argued for the validity of despotism and class differentiation between the monarchs and the subjects and between father and son. They insisted on deepening one's experience of the pre-existing "law" on the basis of knowing by means of investigation of things to reach an understanding the law. Lu Jiuyuan, a scholar of the Southern Song Dynasty, proclaimed that "the universe is my mind and vice versa" and that one should conduct self-examination. His philosophy is called the School of Mind.

Cheng-Zhu Neo-Confucianism emphasized the immutability of the three cardinal guides and five ethical norms to maintain the rule of despots and keep the people in line, which generated adverse influence. However, Neo-Confucianism does attach importance to will, moral integrity, moral character, self-discipline, and working hard, and emphasizes one's social responsibility and historical mission, affirming the dignity of human beings.

Cheng-Zhu Neo-Confucianism built an exquisite, rigid theoretical system that became the mainstream of Confucianism, and had a far-reaching impact on China's political life and cultural education.

In the Song Dynasty, the emerging *Ci* was the mainstream in Chinese literature. *Ci*, also known as "long and short sentences," made it easy to express one's ideas flexibly and could be sung to the accompaniment of music. As with the poetry of the Tang Dynasty, *Ci* poetry was another highlight in ancient Chinese literature. The works of both Su Shi and Xin Qiji were representative of the Heroic School of *Ci* poetry. Su Shi's *Ci* poetry was open and vast in conception, and elegant and unconstrained in tone. The *Ci* poetry of Xin Qiji, who lived in the midst of chaos caused by war in the Southern Song Dynasty, was robust, impassioned, and also plaintive. In the Song Dynasty, the vibrant urban life gave rise to the Gracious School of *Ci* poetry as represented by Liu Yong. His poems, periphrastic and implicit, were so popular that there was a saying that "where there was a well, there were people singing Liu Yong's *Ci* poems."

Li Qingzhao, the most prominent female *Ci* poet of the Song Dynasty, wrote with a distinct style. In the early stage, her poems were happy and joyful, while in the later stage, after the collapse of the state and the bereavement of her husband, they conveyed feelings of homelessness and regrets.

Zaju opera of the Yuan Dynasty combines multiple performing modes to tell a complete story, including poetry and *Ci* poetry, music, dancing, role-playing, singing, and dialogue. A popular form of art, *Zaju* experienced unprecedented development in the period, showing that literature reflective of daily life could become popular. Guan Hanqing was the most famous of all playwrights in the Yuan Dynasty. His representative work, *The Injustice Done to Dou E,* lays bare the official corruption through the injustice done to Dou E, who, grief-stricken, cried out, "Earth! How can you be Earth since you can't tell right from wrong? Heaven! How can you be Heaven since you mistake the good for the guilty?"

Playwright Guan Hanqing.

The Romance of the Western Chamber, written by Wang Shifu, another playwright of the Yuan Dynasty, tells the love story of Zhang Gong and Cui Yingying, conveying the common aspiration of young couples to seek for free love.

The rise of Neo-Confucianism made scholars pay more attention to self-cultivation. As for calligraphy, there were four great calligraphy artists in the Song Dynasty, namely Su Shi, Huang Tingjian, Mi Fu, and Cai Xiang. They admired the calligraphic style of the Wei and Jin Dynasties, stressed personality, ignored rules, and advocated working "with verve and without rules." The landscape paintings of the time focused more on the impressionistic style and were expressive of temperament, verve, and spirit. Among the realistic paintings that showed ordinary life, *Along the River During the Qingming Festival,* by Zhang Zeduan of the Northern Song Dynasty, was the most famous of all. By adopting the "scattered dot" painting technique, the painter vividly reproduced, on a five-meter-long scroll of paper, the prosperous scenes of Bianjing along the Bianhe River at the end of the Northern Song Dynasty, making those who watch it feel as if they were "personally in the bustling crowds in the city of Bianjing."

Yuan Dynasty theater performance, depicted in a mural of Guangsheng Temple in Hongdong, Shanxi.

From the 10th to 13th centuries, Europe was oppressed by feudal land ownership. The serfs were humble in position, and ideology remained fettered by theological obscuration. In contrast, China witnessed three great inventions and their application, as well as a sharp rise in both the urban economy and overseas trade during the Song Dynasty, becoming a leader of the world at the time.

昔人云人芝蘭之室久而忘其香夫芝蘭枝葉之劉美矣世蘭弟
樂也我顏居深山大壑間與夫青莖紫萼互相掩映各正其命酒
為詩曰峀山峻礛見芝蘭竹影縱橫其片席便入乾坤為巨室老夫高
枕臥其間

乾隆年學兄知堂
板橋鄭燮奉寄

Chapter 8

The Ming and Qing Dynasties (before the Opium War): Prosperity of the Farming Civilization and Crisis before Modern Times

Measures to Intensify Imperial Power during the Ming and Qing Dynasties

The Ming and Qing dynasties (before the Opium War) lasted from 1368 to 1840 in Chinese history.

At the end of the Yuan Dynasty (1279–1368), the situation of class differences and national contradictions was deteriorating, which triggered large-scale peasant insurgence. In 1368, Zhu Yuanzhang headed a peasant army to overthrow the Yuan Dynasty, defeat the leaders of other peasant uprisings, and establish the Ming Dynasty with its capital in Yingtian (Nanjing, Jiangsu).

Emperor Taizu (Zhu Yuanzhang) and Emperor Chengzu (Zhu Di) of the Ming Dynasty enforced imperial power by abolishing the prime minister, creating the system of the Grand Secretariat, and setting up secret services to enforce control over grassroots thinking and cultural circles. They moved the capital to Beijing during their reign, formulating the basic structure of the Ming Dynasty system of centralized monarchic despotism. At the same time, the rulers of the early Ming Dynasty implemented economic policies to encourage cultivation of wastelands, reduce corvee and taxes, reward those who planted cash crops, and lift the social status of the craftsmen, which helped recover and develop the economy. The Yongle Period (1403–1424) of Emperor Zhu Di saw

Zhu Yuanzhang, Emperor Taizu of the Ming Dynasty.

social stability and strong national strength and was another prosperous time in Chinese history.

In the early days of the Wanli Period (1573–1620), prime minister Zhang Juzheng reformed the taxation and corvee systems and implemented the Single-Whip Reform to combine original land taxes, corvee, and incidental taxes into one, and levied taxes based on land area. The reform stimulated development of the commodity economy, and more than thirty industrial and commercial cities emerged south of the lower reaches of the Yangtze River. New changes similar to capitalism in western countries appeared in the handicraft workshops.

In the late Ming Dynasty, land mergers deteriorated. Peasants, forced out of their homeland, abandoned a vast amount of land, which deteriorated into wasteland.

At the end of the Ming Dynasty, the invasion of the Late Jin and natural disasters over several consecutive years finally triggered large-scale peasant uprisings that involved millions of people and lasted nearly twenty years. In March 1644, the insurgent peasant army headed by Li Zicheng occupied Beijing, and Emperor Chongzhen committed suicide. The Ming Dynasty came to its end. In April of the same year, the Qing army, which had

Chapter 8   The Ming and Qing Dynasties (before the Opium War)

The Ming Tombs. Thirteen emperors of the Ming Dynasty are buried there.

arrived at Shanhaiguan Pass, managed to summon Wu Sangui, commander of Ningyuan of the Ming Dynasty, to surrender and conquered the insurgent peasant army. Thereafter, the Qing moved the capital from Shengjing (Shenyang, Liaoning) to Beijing in September, seizing the supreme dominion of the country.

The Manchu, who established the Ming Dynasty, were a new federation of ethnic groups formed after Nurhachi unified the Jurchen tribes during the late Ming Dynasty. Nurhachi proclaimed himself Khan and established a kingdom named Late Jin. His son Huangtaiji ascended the throne and proclaimed himself emperor in Shengjing and changed the title to Qing. After entering Shanhaiguan Pass, the Qing army seized land on a large scale, forced the poor to be their servants, and compelled the residents in southeastern coastal areas to move inward 30 to 50 *li*. They also forced the Han people to shave their hair and braids with the threat that "if you want to live, you must

Portrait of Emperor Kangxi.

cut your hair; if you keep your hair, you will be killed" to follow the system of the Qing, making it a symbol of the reign of Manchu nobility. The policies of ethnic group oppression and the backwardness of the production relationship implemented in the early Qing Dynasty worsened the social economy, already seriously damaged by years of civil war. The trend of evolving into a modern society was interrupted.

　The cruel policies implemented in the early Qing Dynasty aroused fierce resistance. Campaigns against the Qing rulers sped their demise. The basic crisis, a separation between the land and the laborers at the end of the Ming Dynasty, was removed via peasant warfare. This created a favorable environment for economic recovery in the early Qing Dynasty. During the reigns of

Chapter 8   The Ming and Qing Dynasties (before the Opium War)

The Military Affairs Division.

Emperor Kangxi, Emperor Yongzheng, and Emperor Qianlong, the social economy developed rapidly and reached a new height in the history of China.

The Ming and Qing dynasties saw further strengthened centralism and highly inflated imperial power.

The Six-Department System from the Sui and Tang dynasties remained basically unchanged during the Ming and Qing dynasties, while the Three-Ministry System was adjusted and reformed to further reduce the power of the prime ministers and to reinforce the power of the emperor.

During the period of Hongwu (1368–1398) in the early Ming Dynasty, the *Zhongshu* Ministry was cancelled, and the post of prime minister was removed. The emperor was in direct charge of the six departments and handled state affairs in person. Zhu Yuanzhang set up the position of *Diange Daxueshi* (Imperial Grand Scholar) to help him handle state affairs and documents. The cabinet system was developed during the Yongle Period (1403–1424). In the early Ming Dynasty, the cabinet had no power to decide state affairs independently and functioned only as an assistant to the emperor. But the power of *Daxueshi* (Grand Scholar) became increasingly strong, and the cabinet head resembled the prime minister of earlier times.

Emperor Yongzheng of the Qing Dynasty set up the Military Affairs Division. A hub from which the emperor could issue orders and handle state affairs, the division took part in discussions on all critical state affairs, such as the military and administrative programs, civil and diplomatic affairs, including official promotions, removals, assignments, and important case hearings, and drafted orders for the emperor.

The ministers of the Military Affair Division were, however, of lower rank, with no dedicated government office or subordinates, and were forbidden from contacting officials without authorization. All reports submitted by the officials were presented directly to the Emperor, then forwarded to the Military Affairs Division to ensure that the will of the emperor was followed. The decision-making and administration system centered on the emperor was efficient and confidential, enabling the emperor to maximize his control over the political situation and state affairs.

The control of the central government over local areas was beefed up during the Ming and Qing dynasties. In the Ming Dynasty, the *Buzhengshi* Division was set up to manage the provincial administrative affairs. The *Tixing Anchasi* and *Duzhihui* divisions were set up to manage criminal law, and military and administrative affairs, respectively. The three divisions, as offices of the central government in the provinces, were independent from one other. Their officials discussed all critical issues before reporting to the central government, facilitating vertical leadership.

In the Qing Dynasty, in addition to the viceroy who governed one or several provinces, a *Xunfu* (governor) was set up in the provinces to take charge of administrative affairs. The viceroy and Xunfu were favorites of the emperor and had the right to send confidential reports to the emperor. Sometimes the viceroy and Xunfu would be based in the same city and kept one another in check. Their tenure was not long, facilitating the control of the emperor.

The Ming and Qing dynasties also promoted reform in the southwestern areas. They dismissed the hereditary *Tusi* and appointed officials called *Liuguan* to manage local administration in a style similar to that of the central plains. The Qing Dynasty set up a "general" in the northwestern and northeastern areas, respectively, to handle military and administrative affairs and enforce control.

In the Ming and Qing dynasties, the supervision system became even more rigid. *Duchayuan* was set up at the central level and was responsible for inspecting and impeaching the officials. Duchayuan appointed censors to supervise the local officials. Corresponding to the six departments, six special divisions were set up to inspect the six departments and rectify their malpractices. The supervision system played an active role in cracking down on separatist forces, rectifying the official administration, punishing corruption, improving administrative efficiency, and consolidating centralist rule. However, the focus of the supervision system in the Ming and Qing dynasties was on assessing the loyalty of officials, not on assessing their job performance. Hence, there was little supervision of and constraints applied to the decision-making process of the emperor.

Chapter 8　The Ming and Qing Dynasties (before the Opium War)　　**151**

Wooden seal of the *Jinyiwei* of the Ming Dynasty.

In the Ming and Qing dynasties, the kinship-based clan organizations were widely established in rural areas. The wide control net formed by *Bao-jia* (neighborhood administrative system) and clan organizations extended even to remote areas and became a powerful tool for the rulers to control the population.

In the early Ming Dynasty, the emperors set up *Jinyiwei* (Brocade-Clad Guards) and the *Dong Chang* (secret police). The two organizations were authorized to detect and investigate crimes via torture and killing. To establish

The Palace Museum in Beijing is the imperial palace of the Ming and Qing dynasties. Pictured is the Taihe Palace, where the emperors' court ceremonies were held.

FYI — FOR YOUR INFORMATION

THE POLITICAL SYSTEM OF ANCIENT CHINA

The political system of ancient China featured precise specialization and functional division, and was managed by professional bureaucrats based on rational established rules and precedents. In many aspects, China was well-equipped with conditions for its transformation to a modern one, but its very perfection gave rise to arrogance and almost excluded the possibility of change.

—Gilbert Rozman, *The Modernization of China*

the absolute authority of the imperial power, the Ming Dynasty also instituted the *Tingzhang* System, whereby the emperors could arbitrarily flog any minister who they found unsatisfactory at the imperial court. The relationship between the king and his ministers became one of a master and his slaves.

The centralized regime of the ancient China was well organized and contributed to efficient management of a vast territory and a large population by professional bureaucrats selected via the imperial examination system. The regime was of great significance as it promoted the formation of a multi-ethnic nation and boosted economic and cultural development for a long time. However, the separation of power in ancient China was merely a form of check and balance under imperial power and it could not veto the emperor. It was merely a supplement to the rule of absolute monarchy.

Consolidation and Development of a Unified Multi-ethnic Country

The Ming and Qing dynasties (before the Opium War) witnessed unprecedented consolidation and development of China as a unified multi-ethnic country.

In the early 16th century, the western colonial forces rapidly expanded into the eastern world following Portugal and Spain's successful opening of the navigation routes. In 1548, troops of the Ming Dynasty heavily defeated the invading Portuguese fleet in Shuangyu near Ningbo, Zhejiang, burning seventy-seven battleships of different sizes. After that incident, the Portuguese employed means of deceit and bribery, saying their commercial ships had suffered windstorm, and were thus permitted to set up sheds in Macao to rest and dry their clothes. They went on to build ramparts, barbettes, and official mansions on the pretext of defending the invasion of the Dutch. In 1621, the Ming government destroyed the Qingzhou city built by the Portuguese, and levied an annual tax of 20,000 taels of silver upon the Portuguese in Macao. That paved the way for Macao's later development into a colonial site, though the Ming Dynasty still had sovereignty over Macao.

In the middle Ming Dynasty, Japanese warriors, merchants, and pirates often harassed the southeastern coastal areas. They even once attacked Shanghai and Suzhou and finally reached Nanjing. In 1555, Qi Jiguang was entrusted to resist the Japanese pirates in eastern Zhejiang. He won nine battles in Taizhou and drove the Japanese pirates away in 1565.

In 1598, the Spanish attacked Guangdong, building houses at Hutiaomen. But their houses were later burnt down by the Ming troops, and the Spanish were chased out of Chinese territory.

In 1642, Dutch colonists invaded and occupied Taiwan, where they cruelly exploited the Taiwanese and their resources. In 1661, Zheng Chenggong, who had initiated wars against the Qing Dynasty in southeastern coastal areas, led a troop of 25,000 soldiers and hundreds of battleships to cross the straits eastward from Jinmen, successfully capturing Chiqian City, the strategic site of the Dutch troops. After another eight months of siege, he launched a fierce attack and finally forced

Statue of Zheng Chenggong on the Gulangyu Islet.

Frederick Coyett, the Dutch Governor, to sign a document of surrender. Zheng's successful reoccupation of Taiwan checked the further eastward expansion of the western colonists, ensured the stability of China's southeastern provinces, and played an indirect role in protecting other Asian countries.

In the 1640s, Russian troops launched large-scale invasions into the mainland of China, occupying such northeastern areas as Yakesa and Nerchinsk. They brazenly plundered the areas, severely infringing upon the sovereignty of the Qing Dynasty and endangering both life and property. Qing troops waged two counterattacks in Yakesa in 1685 and 1686, defeating the Russian troops, who were forced to agree to a peace talk with only dozens of remaining soldiers. In 1689, both parties signed the Treaty of Nerchinsk, finalizing Qing sovereignty over the drainage areas of the Heilong and Wusuli rivers, including Kuyedao (Sakhalin Island). The treaty also provided that traveling businessmen of both countries could cross the borders for trade by presenting their passports. After the signing of the Treaty of Nerchinsk, the eastern part of the border areas between China and Russia enjoyed a relatively peaceful and stable situation that greatly facilitated bilateral trade.

The Great Wall of the Ming Dynasty stretches from the Yalu River in the east to Jiayu Pass in the west, and is 6,350 kilometers long.

Chapter 8 The Ming and Qing Dynasties (before the Opium War)

The period from the Ming Dynasty to the early Qing saw effective counterattacks for safeguarding sovereignty, as well as zigzag but generally upward development in border areas where ethnic groups lived.

In the early Ming Dynasty, the remaining forces of the Yuan Dynasty that retreated to the Mongolian Plateau launched constant military attacks against the southern areas. In the middle of the Ming Dynasty, Wala unified all the Mongolian tribes, defeating a 500,000-soldier troop of the Ming Dynasty at Tumubao. He captured Emperor Yingzong alive and threatened the capital city of Beijing. In the early Jiajing Period of the Ming Dynasty, the Andahan Tribe of Tatar grew particularly strong. Between the Longqing and Wanli periods, Grand Secretary Zhang Juzheng initiated new reforms in the bordering areas with a view to "increasing the exchanges between the Han and Mongolians externally and reinforcing defensive systems internally." Vigorous efforts were made to amend and cement the Great Wall and consolidate northern border defenses. As a result, Andahan couldn't get through the northern border. His people urgently needed to exchange their goods for the farm produce of the central plains, so he begged for peace talks. The court of the Ming Dynasty accepted his request, conferring the title of King of Shunyi upon Andahan, and agreed to open eleven markets for exchange. From then on, the northern border areas saw a growing population, an increase in reclaimed land, and frequent commodity exchange.

Certain key border towns developed into "pearls at the frontiers" that differed little from the central plains. The Mongolian areas boasted not only a booming stockbreeding sector, but also a fast-developing agriculture, a vast area of reclaimed land, numerous villages, and the rise of Guihua City (present-day Hohhot). The Mongolians and Han people gradually merged with one another in many ways, such as ideology, culture, and folk customs. According to historical records, the Han people "living in bordering areas somewhat looked like the foreign people," and were called "Han aliens" (Han Yi) during the Wanli Period. The Mongolian leaders also practiced the customs of Han, and even "prayed to be a member of Han in the afterlife."

After coming into power in the middle 17th century, Galdan, from Mongolia's Junggar Tribe in the West Desert, constantly launched attacks on its neighboring tribes. He later occupied areas both north and south of the Tianshan mountain range and colluded with the Russians to wage a large-scale rebellion. In 1690, Galdan attacked Inner Mongolia, also threatening to attack Beijing. To maintain national integrity, Emperor Kangxi of the Qing Dynasty personally led his army in war and defeated the rebel forces in Uklark Poktu. Qing troops carried out wars against Galdan and his successors for another seventy years. They eventually destroyed the aristocratic forces of Junggar in 1571 and unified the areas north of the Tianshan mountain range.

The Qing Dynasty established the post of general in Uliastai (present-day Dzhavkhlant, Mongolia) and counselor minister in Hovd (present-day Hovd in Mongolia). It also set up many military sentries, Kalun, along the northern borders, with many posthouses and smooth post roads, intensifying its direct control over the northern border areas. In the meantime, the Qing Dynasty paid great attention to cultivating its popularity among the top leaders of ethnic groups by implementing the policy of "retaining their own customs based on religious beliefs," retaining their jurisdiction over their respective tribes, reducing taxes and tributes, awarding ranks of nobility, and paying high salaries. The royal family of the Qing Dynasty married into the Mongolian noble class. In addition, eleven spectacular Lama temples were built outside the Chengde Imperial Summer Resort. There, royal Mongolians who were designated to visit the emperors of the Qing Dynasty accompanied the emperors to practice martial arts and go hunting. That helped coordinate and develop Qing's relations with all tribes of Mongolia, and helped the Qing Dynasty "rally people of all ethnic groups to consolidate power."

The Imperial Summer Resort and its Outlying Temples at Chengde imitate Tibet's Potala Palace grounds.

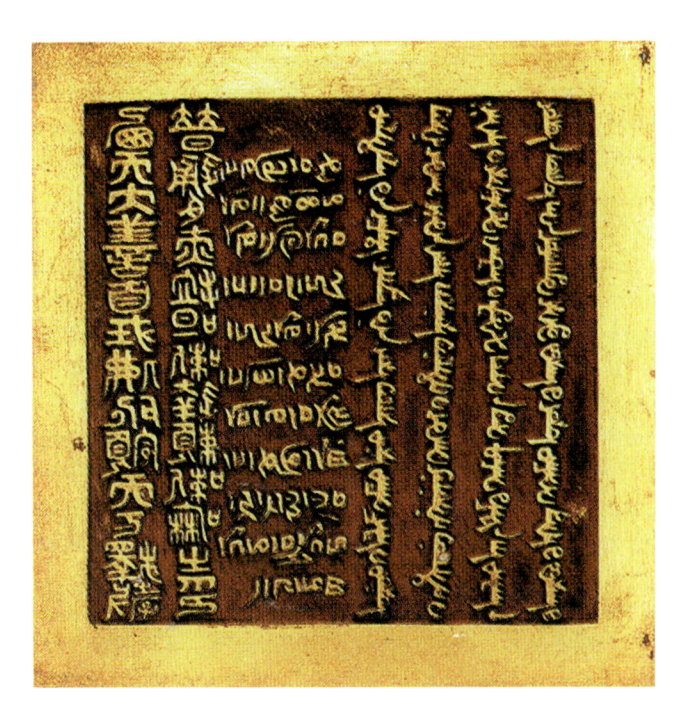

Gold seal granted to the Dalai Lama by the Qing court.

In the early Ming Dynasty, the court set up seven garrisons with Hami as the center to beef up its control over the northwestern borders. In the early Qing Dynasty, the Uygur ethnic group, Islamic converts distributed in areas south of the Tianshan mountain range, were called "Huibu." In 1757, Burhan al-Din and Khwaja Jinan, Huibu nobles, launched rebellions. But their tyranny and despotism made them quickly lose popularity among the people and led to their defeat by the Qing troops. In 1762, after suppressing the rebellion, the Qing Dynasty established the post of general in Yili, thereby putting a person in charge of all military and civil affairs in areas both south and north of the Tianshan mountains. The whole Xinjiang area, including the Balkhash Lake, enjoyed unprecedented peace and stability.

During the Yongle Period of the Ming Dynasty, the court set up Nu'ergan Dusi in Telin, the estuary of the Heilongjiang River, granting jurisdiction over the drainage areas of the Heilongjiang and Wusuli rivers. In 1433, the imperial inspector minister of the Ming Dynasty had the stone tablet "Reconstruction of the Yongning Temple" erected. The tablet recorded details of the court's administration over Nu'ergan Dusi in Han, Mongolian, Jurchen, and Tibetan characters, serving as witness to the joint efforts of all ethnic groups in developing the northeastern areas.

Telin is where the Manchu people rose and later replaced the Ming Dynasty with the Qing Dynasty. In the early Qing Dynasty, the post of general was established in Fengtian, in Jilin, and in Heilongjiang to strengthen Qing's patrol and defense along the Sino-Russian border and to check Russian invasions. That ensured stability and safety in the border areas and led to unprecedented development in Northeast China.

Tibet accepted the jurisdiction of the Ming Dynasty after the Yuan Dynasty ended. The court sent troops on several occasions to put down rebellions plotted by Junggar nobles and to defeat the invading Gurkha tribe. Emperor Shunzhi of the Qing Dynasty formally conferred the title of Dalai Lama upon the Fifth Dalai. Emperor Kangxi later conferred the title of Panchen Erdini upon the Fifth Panchen. In 1727, the Ming court set up the post of Minister to Tibet. In 1793, an imperial decree was issued, stipulating that the rights of official appointment and removal, administrative, financial, military, and foreign affairs of Tibet were under the Minister to Tibet.

Emperor Qianlong further formulated the "Golden Vase Lottery" system, ordering that candidates for the reincarnated Living Buddha of Lamaism must be supervised by the Minister to Tibet and be determined by drawing lots in the golden vase awarded by the court. Those measures helped stabilize the political situation in Tibet, pushed forward the local economy, and further made Tibet an inalienable part of China.

The Ming and Qing dynasties adopted the policy of "changing tribal authorities to regular officials" in southwestern areas, abolishing the post of Tusi and implementing a regime system identical to those of inland areas. Furthermore, efforts were made to register households and population, measure land and reclaim barren fields, sort coins and grains, exempt Tusi's miscellaneous taxes and duties, build roads, and set up schools. Advanced production techniques were also introduced from the inland areas, promoting local economic growth.

After a century-long struggle against invasions from the outside and rebel forces from within, the Qing Dynasty finally founded a unified and consolidated country. Its vast territory stretched from Balkhash Lake and Congling in the west, to the Sea of Okhotsk and Sakhalin Island in the east, and extended from Siberia in the north, to the Paracel Islands and Spratly Islands in the south, and to Taiwan and other islands in the southeast—which basically laid a foundation for China's present territory. Some neighboring countries as well were subject to or were tributary states of the Qing Dynasty.

There were great advancements in the border areas during the first half of the Qing Dynasty. During the reign of Emperor Qianlong, the agricultural produce of northeastern China not only supplied local needs, but was

Gold cup inlaid with treasures, Qing Dynasty, from the Palace Museum in Beijing.

also transported to inland areas. The four cities of Qiqi Ha'er, Mo'ergen, Hulan, and Heilongjiang boasted grain storage of up to 450,000 *dan*. Since the late Ming Dynasty, some key towns in the border areas between Han and Mongolia, such as Zhangjiakou, saw the emergence of various shops, including silk, cloth, wool, and grocery shops, that extended four or five *li*. Areas north of the Tianshan mountains boasted up to 560,000 *mu* of military agricultural colonies during the the mid-reign period of Emperor Qianlong alone. In particular, Yili was a place "where there were vast numbers of immigrants from inland areas, densely distributed villages, herds of sheep and horses, and crowds of merchants. Even the best of Shaoxing and Kunqu Opera could be seen there."

The formation and development of China as a unified multi-ethnic country was not only reflected in definite political accord, consolidated military defenses in border areas, and mutual economic dependency between inland and bordering areas, but also in harmonious relations among ethnic groups as well as close cultural exchanges.

At a critical time during the resistance of the Russian invasion, Kerk Mongolia was completely defeated due to a sudden attack from Galdan of the Junggar Tribe. When discussing the solution, the top Mongolian leaders said, "Russians never embrace Buddhism, and they have customs, languages, and clothes different from ours, so mixing with the Russians is not a strategy for long-term stability. If we emigrate to the inland areas and submit to the Emperor of the Ming Dynasty, we could enjoy a happy life for thousands of years."

In the third year of the reign of Emperor Chongzhen of the Ming Dynasty (1630), the Turehot Tribe, which had been forced by Junggar to move to areas around the Volga River, began their journey back to the motherland in 1770 after experiencing a great deal of hardship and difficulties. These examples show that only when the nomadic economy at the frontiers was combined with a commodity economy typical of the central plains and areas south of the Yangtze, and when all ethnic groups merged with one another based on a shared mutual culture, did the vast expanses of the border areas become part of a unified multi-ethnic country.

Prosperity of Farming Civilization and Embryonic Modern Industry

The period from the 13th to 18th centuries, the heyday of the Ming and Qing dynasties, witnessed great advances in agriculture and all-around development in both social and economic fields.

In the second half of the Ming Dynasty, the Single-Whip Reform was implemented, integrating the original land taxes, corvee, and incidental taxes into one. Taxes were levied based on land area alone. The reform stimulated development of the commodity economy, and some rich people even abandoned their land and engaged in commercial business. In the early Qing Dynasty, the reform of Substitution of Farming Land Tax for Poll Tax, adopted to levy taxes only according to land area, completely canceled the poll tax and weakened personal bondage. That marked the maturity of the ancient tax system and a significant renovation in treatment of the working class.

There was an obvious progression in management and production techniques. *The Exploitation of the Work of Nature,* written at the end of the Ming Dynasty, covered about thirty techniques in both industrial and agricultural production, gaining for China a leading position in the world. Two-season rice was promoted and per unit production increased significantly. The introduction and expanded planting area of high-yield plants such as corn and sweet potato, in addition to the widespread planting of cotton, significantly increased food and clothing options. The big increase in grain output not only satisfied the needs of the growing population, but also facilitated the cultivation of economic crops, paving the way for a flow of people from the agricultural sector to the handicraft sector, altering the traditional economy.

Chapter 8 The Ming and Qing Dynasties (before the Opium War)   **161**

Images of the Imperial Capital (part) portrays Beijing in the mid-Ming Dynasty.

The Prosperity of the Southern Capital (part) depicts the serried stores and prosperity of Nanjing in the mid-Ming Dynasty.

During the Ming and Qing dynasties, the market-responsive private handicraft sector grew rapidly, replacing government-operated workshops.

Commodity circulation expanded in the middle Ming Dynasty. Silver was the major currency, and commercial capital became increasingly active. Businessmen with huge sums of money traded and transported bulk commodities across the country, and became more deeply involved in production.

In the middle and late Ming Dynasty, some distribution centers for handicrafts and raw materials that appeared in areas along the Grand Canal and south of the Yangzte developed into industrial and commercial cities. Clusters of numerous merchants and intermediary businessmen proliferated; they introduced deals for sellers and buyers and appraised commodity quality and prices. In Suzhou, Songjiang, Hangzhou, Jiaxing, and Huzhou alone, the more than 30 cities and towns of the middle Ming Dynasty increased to more than 200 in the early Qing Dynasty.

The national strength of the Ming and Qing dynasties was particularly reflected in its expanding farmland and growing population. Total area of farmed land rose from 850 million *mu* in the Ming Dynasty to around 1 billion *mu* in the Qing Dynasty. The registered population surged from 66 million in the early Ming Dynasty to more than 100 million at its end, and reached 410 million in 1840, the 20th year of the reign of Qing Emperor Daoguang.

From 1720 to 1820, the proportion of China's GDP in the world's total increased at a rate far higher than that of all European countries combined. At the beginning of the 19th century, six of the world's ten cities with 500,000 or more residents were in China. From the middle and late Ming Dynasty to the early Qing Dynasty, half of the world's total silver output flew into China. China was a major center of world economy and trade.

A new form of business operation known as workshop handicraft emerged in some economically developed areas in the middle Ming Dynasty. Historical records show that in the Wanli Period, most households in Suzhou were employed in silk weaving, and "most of the households in the northeast city were workshop owners." The presence of detailed division of labor, such as weaver, damask worker, yarn worker, dyer, and cartwright, indicate that production had reached a certain size and had a relatively high technique. The record that "the workshop owners provide the fund while the workers labor" indicates a pure employment relationship.

The workshop owners provided production materials and wages, "paying by day or hour," and the laborers enjoyed personal freedom. Records showing employees "as common people who earn their own livings" and "asking others who haven't been employed to substitute for them in case of absence due to particular reasons" also indicate that employees had personal freedom. In Suzhou, in addition to weavers who worked for the same employer all the time, temporary craftsmen went to different sites according to their particular specialties, and waited for employment from the big employers. Hence, there was a functioning job market.

This way of doing business featured a division of labor and a high degree of socialization and working efficiency. It represents qualitative changes when compared to traditional government-operated workshops and small private workshops. Private businesses that earned added profit from labor encouraged free employment, an indicator of the early emergence of capitalism.

The Tongsheng Well Contract (1779) in the reign of Emperor Qianlong of the Qing Dynasty, and the Tianyuan Well Contract (1796) in the reign of Emperor Jiaqing, show that business forms such as a joint partnership, "sharing responsibilities and profits based on respective shares," had already been adopted in the production of salt in Zigong, Sichuan, showing signs of the modern stock system.

The changes that differentiated the economy of the late Ming and Qing dynasties from previous economic modes indicate that the overdeveloped agricultural sector had been changing all along. Rise of the new elements had paved the way for the evolution of a civilization based on industry.

Culture of the Ming and Qing Dynasties: A Mixture of Old and New

The Ming and Qing dynasties saw drastic changes in Chinese society and were a turning point of great historical significance. Extraordinarily sharp contradictions and conflicts between old and new forces resulted in a pattern of intertwining new and old elements in science and ideology.

The development of a commodity economy triggered the demand for renovated techniques, promoted scientific and technological growth, and gave rise to a number of scientists who made breakthroughs in traditional scientific fields.

An Outline Treatise of Medical Herbs, written by Li Shizhen of the late Ming Dynasty, covers an extensive range of subjects, including medicine, pharmacy, biology, chemistry, mineralogy, geology, and phenology. He initiated the classification methods for Chinese medicines, categorizing them in the inorganic sphere, plant sphere, and animal sphere based on the principle of "from small to big" and "from humble to noble"—a system that clearly incorporates the ideas of biological evolution. Li also pointed out the similarities between apes and human beings. Darwin cited parts of the book that dwell on the seven species of chicks and the domestication of goldfish in his argument for "the

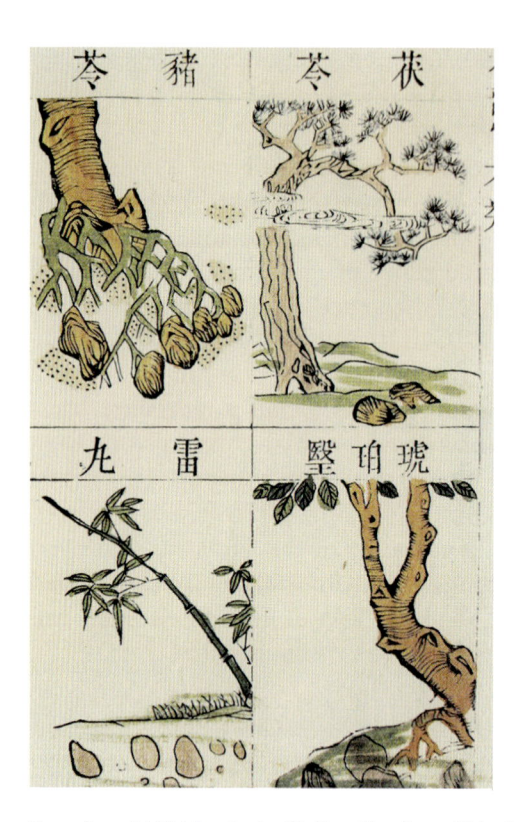

Page from Li Shizhen's *An Outline Treatise of Medical Herbs.*

differentiation occurring in the domestication of animals and plants." Li was the first to bring forward the idea of the "brain being the house of original spirit," saying human thoughts were the function and product of brains, which is of great significance.

The Exploitation of the Work of Nature, an encyclopedia of Chinese science written in the 17th century, covers all major industrial techniques of the time, including those of agriculture, textiles, mining, metallurgy, chemical engineering, boat building, and weaponry; it also contains bibliographies of Chinese and non-Chinese sources, a glossary, and appendices on Chinese dynasties, measurements, and transmission of techniques to the West. Compiled by Song Yingxing in the late period of the Ming Dynasty, the encyclopedia has been translated into Japanese, English, German, French, Italian, Russian, and other languages.

Zhu Zaiyu, a descendant of the royal family of the late Ming Dynasty, resigned from his office on seven occasions in order to commit himself to scientific research. He proposed the thought of "principles reflected by numbers

Page from *The Exploitation of the Work of Nature.*

and numbers from principles" and created the Twelve-tone Equal Temperament, solving the theoretic problem of achieving tone change in musical instruments that puzzled people for more than 2,000 years. Joseph Needham (1900–1995) called him "a man from the times of Renaissance although he is far away from Europe."

In *An Agricultural Encyclopedia,* Xu Guangqi of the Ming Dynasty not only summarized previous and current achievements, but also incorporated ideas and methods from western agricultural science and technologies based on long-term experiments. As "the first to introduce the western science," Xu is reputed to be an epoch-making Chinese scientific pioneer in modern history for his spotlight on mathematical research and persistence in investigation, experiment, observation, and summary, all elements of modern scientific research.

Xu Xiake's *Travel Diaries,* published in the late years of the reign of Emperor Chongzhen of the Ming Dynasty, is distinctive from common travel notes in many aspects, such as his descriptions of igneous rock, terrestrial heat and springs, the erosive effect of flowing water on rocks, and the dependency of

Xu Guangqi and Italian missionary Matteo Ricci.

plants on climate. His scientific investigation, featuring precise description and in-depth analysis, paved the way for research in natural science. In 1953, the Chinese Academy of Science re-investigated the fifteen water-eroded caves that he once explored and drew roughly similar data. Joseph Needham appraised his traveling dairies as "having amazing capability in analyzing various sorts of landforms and employing a wide range of jargon in a very systematic way," and added that the book "reads more like investigative records finished by a field explorer in the 20th century than something written by a scholar in the 17th century."

The multitude of scientists who emerged in the late Ming Dynasty paid greater attention to experiments and mathematical methods typical of modern scientific research. Generally speaking, however, science and technology in the Ming and Qing dynasties lagged far behind that of the West. The high-handed cultural policy and the highly stereotyped and rigid writing style adopted for the imperial examination only exacerbated the situation, leading to an increasingly wide gap between China and the West.

The Ming and Qing dynasties exercised tight control over the ideological and cultural fields, and, in the early Qing, literary inquisitions in particular were frequently used to crack down on opponents and keep thoughts under control. People would be questioned, condemned, and sent to jail for reasons of boldly discussing political affairs and encroaching upon the dignity of emperors. For instance, Wang Xihou, an official candidate in the imperial examination from Jiangxi, was beheaded, as were all of his seven descendents because, in his book, he failed to refer properly to the posthumous titles of the three emperors, including Kangxi. Hai Chengyin, the provincial governor of Jiangxi, was sentenced to death on probation for weak supervision, and another two officials were also suspended from duty for not pointing out the "false" parts. These cruel literary inquisitions forced intellectuals to divorce their commentaries from real life and to engage in writing books with obsolete thought to protect themselves.

In the Ming and Qing dynasties, Neo-Confucianism had occupied a dominant position in the official ideology. The examinations focused on the Four Books and Five Classics. The Four Books refer to *The Great Learning, The Doctrine of the Mean, The Confucian Analects,* and *The Works of Mencius.* The Five Classics include *The Book of Odes, The Book of History, The Book of Changes, The book of Rites,* and *The Spring and Autumn Annals.* All are classic books of Confucians. The answers had to be based on the notes and commentaries of Zhu Xi. Personal views could not be aired, and the writing style was rigid, composed of eight parts called "Eight-part Essay" or "Stereotyped Writing." The imperial examinations, to a great extent, evolved into a tool of the court to bring the people's thoughts under strict control.

Xie Jishi, a censor during the reign of Emperor Yongzheng, was condemned as "unscrupulous" and exiled to the border areas because he made notes to the Neo-Confucian books in a way different from those of Cheng and Zhu. Such cultural depotism led to a depressing situation among intellectuals and seriously hindered scientific and cultural growth.

The Ming and Qing dynasties witnessed both huge changes and intertwining contradictions of all sorts. On the one hand, despotic rule increased and ritual norms became more and more rigid. On the other hand, the ruling class grew extremely corrupt. Political and religious situations got out of control. The peasants uprising at the end of the Ming Dynasty increased public suspicion of and criticism of the despotism and established rules. The emergence of new economy and the introduction of modern western science in the middle Ming Dynasty offered fresh impetus to cultural renovation. Some enlightened intellectuals at the turn of the Ming and Qing dynasties, responding to the new commodity economy, initiated a wave of enlightenment that called for personal liberation, equality, and democracy.

Li Zhi of the Ming Dynasty, famous for his heterodoxy, lashed out at the Cheng-Zhu Neo-Confucianism being promoted by the ruling class, and denied the claim that the doctrines of Confucianism and Mencius were the best. In his eyes, Confucius was not a saint, but "a common person" and the Four Books and Five Classics should not be the only standards for thinking. Li said every person had unique motives and "individual habits in dressing and eating reflect the relations among people." It is a natural gift to seek material pleasure and every one can follow one's nature to emancipate one's personality.

During the turn of the Ming and Qing dynasties, great thinkers included Wang Fuzhi, Huang Zongxi, and Gu Yanwu. Wang Fuzhi emphasized that natural laws are embodied in the material world, and these laws could be correctly understood through observation. His philosophy toppled the theoretic foundation of apriorism of Cheng-Zhu Neo-Confucianism. He also confirmed the rationality of emotional desire and selfish desire as natural instincts of human beings.

Huang Zongxi alleged in public that, "the emperor is the biggest bane of the world." In his philosophy, the ruler and the subject were not master and servant, but equal teacher and friend, completely denying the obsolete ethical norms of the time. He also advocated substituting "the laws of the world enabling every person to get their own share" for "the single law of a family" that binds everybody, so as constrain the rule of the emperor.

In view that scholars addicted to reading the annotations of Cheng (Cheng Hao and Cheng Yi) and Zhu (Zhu Xi) were seriously removed from reality, Gu Yanwu exclaimed that "every person is responsible for the rise and fall of the world." He insisted on being pragmatic and caring about the national economy and people's livelihood, and being dedicated to social reform.

The thinkers during the Ming and Qing dynasties also put forward diverse theories and assumptions about restricting imperial power. The most prominent concept was to advocate freedom of speech, and to establish bottom-to-top supervision mechanisms to ensure clean politics, proper decisions, and social stability.

The progressive thinkers criticized Neo-Confucianism using an unprecedented incisive style of writing, initiating a wave of progressive thinking characterized by profound and novel philosophical concepts, political insight, and a practical, critical spirit. Their thoughts had a tremendous, centuries-long enlightening influence and gave great inspiration to later generations.

In the Ming and Qing dynasties, commercial and industrial towns developed, and the citizen class that emerged promoted the development of literature. Chapter-style novels, developed from play scripts of the Song and Yuan dynasties, focused on narration and mirrored people's lives and social reality. Novels became the mainstream literature.

Of the great literary classics that gained nationwide popularity during the Ming Dynasty, *The Romance of the Three Kingdoms*, written by Luo Guanzhong, was the first full-length historical novel in Chinese history. *The Water Margin*, written by Shi Nai'an, was the first heroic and martial art novel. *The Journey to the West,* written by Wu Cheng'en, typified the genre of immortal beings. *The Golden Lotus,* written by Xiaoxiaosheng from Lanling, was an exemplary novel that describes the ways of life and the changes in social customs. Popular short stories that feature ordinary citizens during the late Ming Dynasty vividly describe the life experiences and pursuits of common people, accurately reflecting the social reality of the time.

The Qing Dynasty saw the emergence of a number of great critical works. *A Dream of Red Mansions,* written by Cao Xueqin, is the best of these. The book focuses on the tragic love story of Jia Baoyu and Lin Daiyu, and presents the general condition of society through the rise and fall of a noble family. While the plots in the novel are complicated, the narrative threads are clear-cut. The language is concise and vivid, the characters lively and full of personality. The book is recognized by many as the pinnacle of China's classic novels.

The Grand View Garden (part) drawn by a Qing dynasty artist according to *A Dream of Red Mansions.*

In addition, *The Strange Stories from a Chinese Studio,* written by Pu Songling, is "a book of indignation" aimed to express the author's dissatisfaction with social darkness. *The Scholars,* written by Wu Jingzi, reveals and satirizes the ugly side of society.

Painters with highly developed personal styles emerged in the Ming and Qing dynasties. Bold and unconstrained, their works stood in sharp contrast to traditional Chinese paintings.

Among these painters, the eight famous reclusive artists and Shi Tao were all clansmen of the Ming Emperor, and became monks after the Ming Dynasty was destroyed. Through calligraphy and paintings, they expressed their experience of life and their sorrow over the destroyed old dynasty. In the mid-Qing Dynasty, eight artists, known as the Eight Eccentrics of Yangzhou, broke conventional rules in painting and manifested works that expressed their sharply defined personalities. Most of their works were impressionistic in style and focused on flowers and birds. As one of the eight eccentrics, Zheng Xie, alias Zheng Banqiao, was good at painting orchids and bamboo.

In the middle and late period of the Ming Dynasty, Kunqu Opera—which combines poetry, music, singing, dance, and drama—prevailed on both sides of the Yangtze River. It developed into an opera performed nationwide, and is called "the origin of all kinds of opera." Kunqu Opera features elegant lyrics and sweet soothing tunes accompanied by pauses. Ming performers sang and danced; soft dance and gentle arias were combined to amuse the ears and eyes of the audience.

Anhui Opera took a dominant role during the reign of Emperor Qianlong of the Qing Dynasty by absorbing singing and performing styles from Hubei Han Tune, Kunqu Opera, Qinqiang melody, and Bangzi melody. On such a basis, a new form of opera—Peking Opera—came into shape in Beijing. Peking Opera is integrated with the essence of ancient opera art and presents an almost perfect artistic pattern. By using artistic means of singing, speaking, gestures, and acrobatics, performers are able to represent the society at large on a small stage.

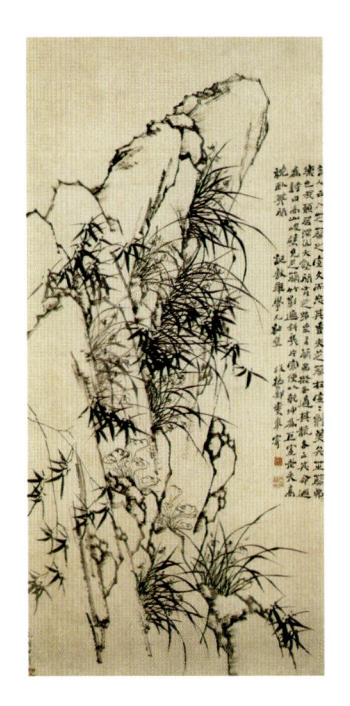

Orchids and Bamboos by Zheng Banqiao in the Qing Dynasty.

Chapter 8 The Ming and Qing Dynasties (before the Opium War)

Thirteen Top Performers: a vivid portrayal of famous Peking Opera actors/actresses of the Tongzhi and Guangxu Periods

Peking Opera took the distinctive Chinese opera to a new level and continues to shine in the hall of human culture.

Crisis before Modern Times

During the Ming and Qing dynasties, the historical development of the world experienced significant changes. One after another, the main European countries leaped from early capitalism to capitalist class revolution and embarked on the road to modern industrial civilization.

The Chinese empire reached a new height in agricultural civilization and some changes from the traditional mode emerged in the social economy, and intellectual and cultural circles, with a tendency toward industrial civilization. However, when the British capitalist revolution occurred, China was mired in peasant wars at the end of the Ming Dynasty, after which it entered a track completely different from that of western countries.

In western countries, commercial economy replaced the natural economy, industrial production replaced handicraft workshops, state power marked by rule of law replaced the privilege of kings and nobles, reasoning broke the hold of religious doctrines that dated from the Middle Ages, and science overcame ignorance. The industrial revolution helped the western bourgeoisie "create more massive and more colossal productive forces than those created by all preceding generations together." But the Qing monarchs, even during the prosperous era of Emperors Kangxi and Qianlong, knew nothing about the historic transformation caused by the spread of industrial civilization, causing the country to sink into its deepest crisis, a watershed moment when China changed from being a leading world power to being a country stuck in the past.

During the Ming and Qing dynasties, the economic structure, characterized by a combination of farming and weaving and self-sufficiency, still took a dominant role throughout the country, but private handicraft and commercial sectors gained strong momentum. From the late Ming Dynasty onward, social values and morality became money-and benefit–oriented. Thitherto despised businessmen were granted high social status. Even Emperor Yongzheng sighed when he said, "I feel it ridiculous that businessmen top all the professions—and scholars, on the contrary, are located in the lowest positions." Correspondingly, proposals that "handicraft and commerce jointly constitute the foundation of society" and "the rich are those the whole state depends upon" were put forward in the civil society.

Farming and Weaving vividly details ancient China's mode of production with men for farming and women for weaving.

However, the rulers of the Qing Dynasty believed that "one more person engaged in commercial business would reduce one peasant working in the farmland," and thus insisted on implementing the policies of "encouraging all the peasants to commit themselves to farming" and "making both labor and land exhausted." This highly intensive mode of production, which confined vast numbers of excessive labor to limited farmland, significantly dampened the impetus of scientific innovation. The long-term family production structure featuring "man tills and women weaves" also hindered the handicraft development, and froze and consolidated the natural agricultural economy.

The rulers of the Qing Dynasty considered that "mining is bound to result in the gathering of people, which would further lead to turbulence." Therefore, on multiple occasions they issued orders forbidding mining, and imposed redundant and heavy commercial taxes on the activities of businessmen and owners of workshops. Under this policy, businessmen and workshop owners could not increase production by accumulating capital, forcing some commercial capital into land exploitation, which inhibited large-scale industrialization.

While practical study prevailed and western learning gradually flowed into the east, the court of the Qing Dynasty still kept pragmatic knowledge about science and technology at arm's length, continued its system of official selection through stereotyped writing, constrained the people's minds with Neo-Confucianism, and vigorously launched literary inquisitions. This made it difficult for modern elements in political and ideological fields to develop. Instead of using uniform, standardized, and efficient educational selection mechanisms to push for industrialization and social transformation, the Qing Dynasty went against the social trend, stubbornly replicating old bureaucratic and legal systems and seriously hindering the process of modernization.

Before the 16th century, China's ocean navigation and ship-making techniques took a leading position in the world. From 1405 to 1433, the Ming Dynasty sent Zheng He on voyages to Southeastern Asia and the Indian Ocean. Zheng led hundreds of huge ships and thousands of sailors, reaching more than thirty countries in Asia and Africa and increasing friendly exchanges and economic communication. However, the Ming Dynasty characterized this work as "giving more but getting less" and seldom took economic benefits into account. The government forced or supervised the production of most goods for export, which led a vast number of craftsmen to flee, and put an end to the feat of ocean navigation, considering it "bad policy."

The Qing court posed as a Celestial Empire, believing that it "had abundant resources and products and didn't need to exchange goods with alien nations." Meanwhile, it closed its doors to the outside world by prohibiting sea trade and foreign trade, with a view to preventing "alien" invasion and avoiding anti-Qing forces in coastal areas. It closed all the trade ports except the port of Guangzhou, and only allowed the officially franchised organization *Shisan*

Shisan Hang, Guangzhou, where foreign trade was handled in the Qing Dynasty

Hang to manage foreign trade. Though the closed-door policy played a certain role in defending the nation against western colonists, it did not narrow the gap between the west and China. Instead, the policy curbed the development of foreign trade and navigation, and the Qing Dynasty lost an opportunity to tap overseas markets, stimulate capital expansion, and promote industrialization through foreign trade. Instead it fostered stagnation and took China far away from the developmental tide sweeping the world.

After the Ming Dynasty, western Jesuits came to China. They helped spread advanced western science and technologies while preaching, allowing western learning to flow into the eastern world. This offered rare opportunities for China to broaden its horizon and merge into the tide of industrial civilization. Xu Guangqi, at the end of the Ming Dynasty, timely put forward the proposal of "overtaking the western counterparts by learning wildly from the other's strong points and combining them with local features based on assimilation of knowledge." But the rulers of the Qing regime stuck to the idea that China was different from foreign nations, and that all western knowledge originated from Chinese culture. The communication between east and west came to a halt following the exile of the Jesuits during the reign of Emperor Yongzheng.

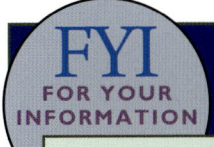

> **FYI — FOR YOUR INFORMATION**
>
> ## DOOMED FATE OF THE QING EMPIRE
>
> A great empire with almost two-thirds of the world's population ignored the changes in the outside world, content with things as they were. Isolated from the rest of the world, its leaders deceived themselves with the illusion that their empire was an extremely perfect one. Such an empire was doomed to lose in the final deadly duel.
>
> —Karl Marx, *History of the Opium Trade*

The rapid growth of capitalism put the entire world into a torrential flow of commodity circulation. Western powers swarmed into other lands across the ocean, plundering valuable resources and objects, trading slaves, and establishing colonial rule. That resulted in a swift change in the balance between western powers and the Qing Empire. During the reign of Emperor Qianlong, George Lord McCartney (1737–1806), an emissary from Britain, once claimed that it would take only several three-mast battleships to destroy the whole coastal fleet of the Qing Dynasty if China were to forbade Sino-British trade or cause severe loss. The seemingly ridiculous prediction did come true, causing Emperor Daoguang to sigh and say, "what a shame it is to not repel the attack of two alien ships! It is no wonder we are despised by the alien nations given our poor military strength."

The first Opium War in 1840 finally disrupted the natural process of China's societal evolution. The Chinese people then faced a solemn and arduous war to gain national independence, and embarked slowly on a complex, twisting, and unique road to modernization.

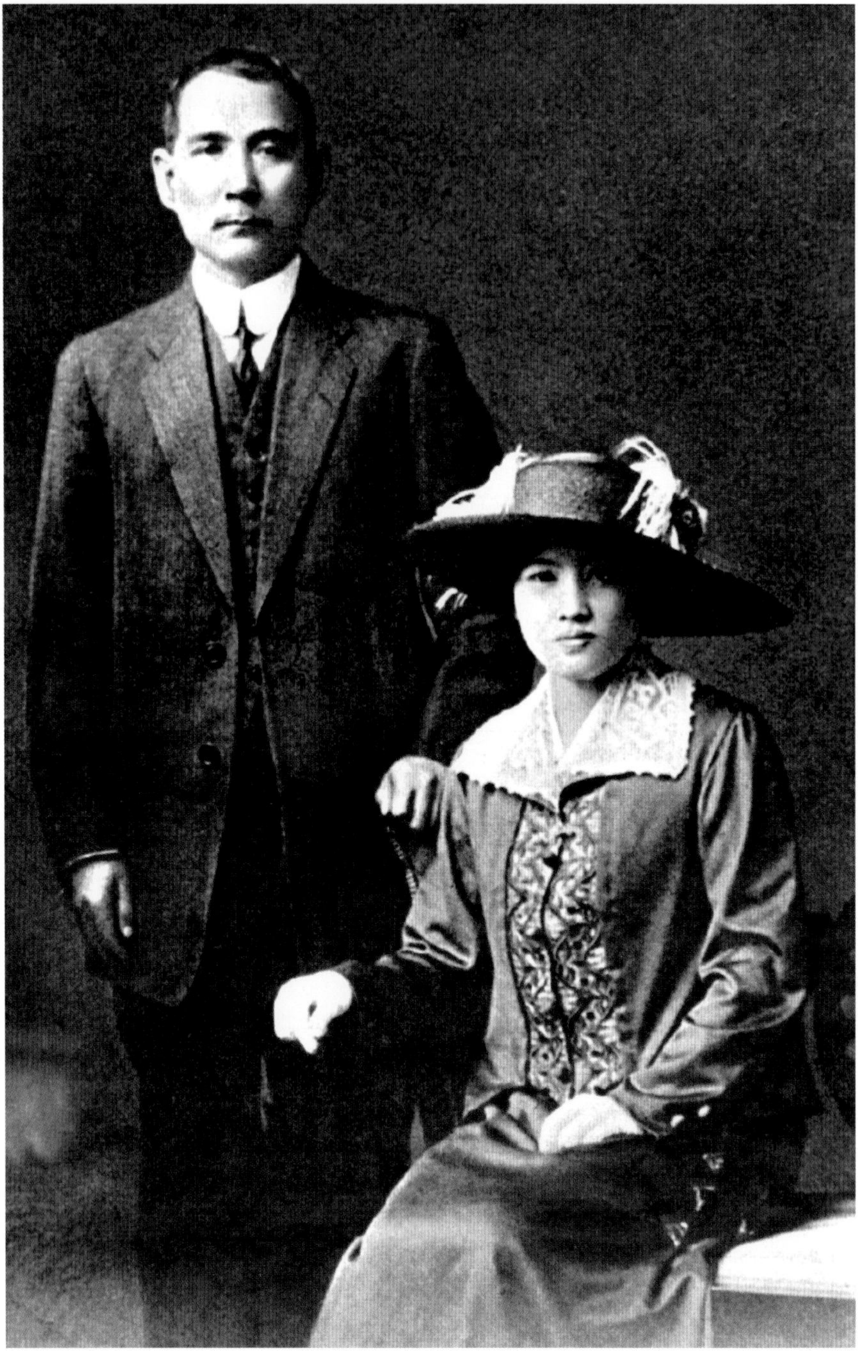

Chapter 9

The Decline and Struggle of Modern China

Western Powers Invade China, and Chinese People Rise in Resistance

In the 16th century, western colonial powers traveled to remote eastern lands to seek resources and to create markets and overseas colonies. In 1514, the Portuguese landed on Chinese land, followed by the Spanish, the Dutch, and the British. In 1793, a British delegation led by McCartney required the Qing imperial court to open trading ports, establish firms, and even to provide Zhoushan Islands for "dry goods." The Qing imperial court determinedly refused the request.

Britain, with a trade deficit against China, began to smuggle opium into the country with intent to seduce Chinese civilians and soldiers to use it. The British government counted on the addictive nature of opium to produce sales that would overturn their trade deficit. The quantity of opium imported reached more than 40,000 chests per year by 1840.

The Chinese people suffered greatly from opium. Had the import continued with no restriction, China would "have had no troops to resist invasion or money to afford the army." Lin Zexu, the government inspector, organized the destruction of captured opium in Humen, Guangzhou, in June 1839. Britain's unconscionable response was to invade China in June 1840, launching the Opium War. China had backward military equipment and was weak in military operations. Moreover, the Emperor of the Qing Dynasty, anxious for a quick victory, quickly turned to compromise and surrender after failing to win within a short time.

Relief: Destroying Opium at Humen.

Therefore, China lost the war. In August 1842, the imperial court of the Qing Dynasty signed the Sino–UK Treaty of Nanking, remising land and paying silver to Britain. The treaty humiliated the nation and forfeited its sovereignty.

In the six decades between the Opium War and the early 1900s, China was invaded and humiliated by foreign powers several times. The Second Opium War, the Sino-French War, the Sino-Japanese War, and the invasion of the Eight-Power Allied Forces all forced the imperial court of the Qing Dynasty to sign a series of unequal treaties. These treaties affected Chinese political,

On August 29, 1842, Chinese and British representatives inked The Sino–UK Treaty of Nanking on board the British vessel Cornwallis.

Ruins of the Yuanmingyuan Garden. The imperial garden of the Qing Dynasty was burned down by the joint Anglo-French army in 1860.

economic, and cultural fields, and infringed on Chinese territorial sovereignty, jurisdiction, and administration. China, temporarily put off the track of independent development, found itself gradually reduced to colonial or semi-colonial status.

When western powers invaded China, they violently disrupted China's chosen isolation from the outside world, and destroyed the country's traditional economy of natural self-sufficiency. They established factories and built railways in China to exploit cheap labor, dump commodities, and plunder resources. At the same time, they spread new social factors, acted unconsciously as a historical tool, and to some extent initiated China's modernization. As western powers attacked China, the national bourgeoisie and proletariat of China came into being. With the bankruptcy of a huge number of farmers, a semi-proletarian class was created.

On Sept. 9, 1945, the official surrender ceremony of Japanese troops in the Chinese Theater was held in Nanjing. Okamura Yasuji, commander-in-chief of the Japanese army, is signing the *Instrument of Surrender*.

FYI — FOR YOUR INFORMATION

GRADUAL COLLAPSE OF THE NATURAL ECONOMY

On the eve of the Opium War, the feudal economy that featured self-sufficiency still played a dominant role in China, even though the early emergence of capitalism cultivated in the Chinese feudal society had grown slowly during centuries of development.

In the wake of the Opium War, one after another treaty ports were opened, resulting in a huge influx of foreign goods. Foreign cotton and cloth replaced local cotton and cloth because of its high quality and low price, making "weaving" separate from "farming" in China. Songjiang and Taicang in Jiangsu were previously the center of China's cotton textile sector and enjoyed a worldwide reputation for clothing and quilting. But "the cloth markets in Songjiang and Taicang shrank significantly" after the Opium War due to the increase in sales of foreign cloth. The textile-dominated rural areas in the southeastern coastal regions suffered huge losses as well; no cotton was available for spinning and no cloth was available for clothing and quilting. Though such phenomena occurred locally, they presaged the collapse of China's natural economy.

Foreign businessmen also bought large quantities of agricultural produce, byproducts, and local specialties from China. They controlled China's export trade in silk and tea, making the production increasingly commercialized, further eroding the base of the natural economy of China.

After World War I, the Japanese consolidated their power in China. In 1931, Japan instigated the Mukden Incident and invaded Northeast China, then instigated the Marco Polo Bridge Incident in 1937, extending its scope of invasion to the whole Chinese territory.

During the fourteen years of the Japanese invasion, Japan turned occupied areas into military and industrial bases to plunder and exploit China's economic resources, calling it "military management" and "consignment operations." The Japanese perpetrated the extremely cruel Nanking Massacre and even used chemical weapons against Chinese citizens. According to statistics, the number of people killed by Japanese invaders was 35 million, the direct economic loss US$100 billion, and indirect economic loss US$500 billion.

During the 100 years after the Opium War, the Chinese people shared a hatred of invading powers and rose to fight. Guan Tianpei and Chen Huacheng heroically guarded cannon stands in the Opium War. Zuo Zongtang fiercely beat down Russian invaders and took back Xinjiang. Feng Zicai led his army to victory in the important battle of Zhennan Pass. Deng Shichang sacrificed his life on the Zhiyuan Battleship fighting against the Japanese army in the Yellow Sea. Soldiers and civilians in Taiwan continued fighting after the Qing imperial court had to remise the land. These heroes represent the brave, fearless fighting spirit of the Chinese.

In August 1945, the Chinese people won the Anti-Japanese War after eight years of fierce fighting, with the support of international anti-Fascist forces.

Democratic Revolutions in Modern China

After the Opium War, Chinese people fought against foreign enemies on the one hand, and on the other struggled to overthrow the Qing imperial court to establish a democratic political system.

Dr. Sun Yat-sen and his wife Soong Ching Ling.

The Taiping Heavenly Kingdom farmers' uprising, which broke out in 1851 and lasted fourteen years, shook the domination of the Qing Empire. When Hong Rengan, one of the rebel army leaders, directed the regime, he imitated western countries and proposed *A New Treatise on Political Counsel,* China's first social reform policy with capitalist features. The policy advanced the democratic process to some extent.

In 1898, the advocates of reform, led by Kang Youwei and Liang Qichao, persuaded Emperor Guangxu of the Qing Dynasty to carry out comprehensive reform. The reform required the setting up of newspaper offices and translation bureaus, freedom of speech, training a new type of navy, transforming the old imperial examination system, establishing new types of schools, transforming the financial system, and planning the national budget and final settlement. However, the reform lasted only 103 days, as the conservatives, led by Empress Cixi, put an end to the process.

Sun Yat-sen, a pioneer of democratic revolution, established the China Revival Society with more than twenty patriotic overseas Chinese in 1894. The organization was the first bourgeoisie revolutionary group in China. From that time onward, China began its bourgeoisie democratic revolution. In 1905, the Chinese Revolutionary League was formally founded and its guiding principle was to "repel foreign invaders, revitalize China, establish a republic, and divide land equally," which was proposed by Sun Yat-sen. He subsequently simplified the guiding principle into the Three People's Principles, namely nationalism, democracy, and the people's livelihood.

On October 10, 1911, the Wuchang Uprising broke out, firing the first shot at the Qing imperial court. In the following months, rebellions flared in all provinces. The Qing Empire disintegrated. Individual independent provinces negotiated and approved the Organization Outlines of the Provisional Government of the Republic of China and the provisional government implemented a presidential republic system.

Chapter 9 The Decline and Struggle of Modern China

On January 1, 1912, Sun Yat-sen was sworn in as the interim President of the Republic of China in Nanjing, marking the founding of the Republic of China. The provisional government in Nanjing put into action the Provisional Constitution of the Republic of China, stipulating that the sovereignty of the Republic of China belonged to all nationals, and citizens had the right to personal freedom, election, participation in political activities, habitation, free speech, publishing, assembly, communication, and freedom of religion. The provisional government issued decrees to announce that the Republic of China would conduct friendly communications with other countries, observe international laws, abolish various taxes, protect national industries, reward overseas Chinese people for domestic investments, and advocate moral education for citizens under the tenets of "freedom, equality, and affection."

On February 12, 1912, Emperor Puyi of the Qing Dynasty announced his abdication, marking the end of the Revolution of 1911. The revolution is of great historical significance in that it overthrew the Qing Empire that had ruled China for more than 200 years, overturned a 2,000-year-old autocratic monarchy, and established a democratic republic.

After the Revolution of 1911, Chinese political fortunes turned. Widespread skirmishes among warlords led to disasters for both the people and the state.

After the victory of the Russian October Revolution in 1917, a number of Chinese intellectuals were attracted to Marxism and Leninism. The May Fourth Movement, aimed at opposing imperialism and feudalism, disseminated the ideas of democracy and science, further helping to blend Marxism

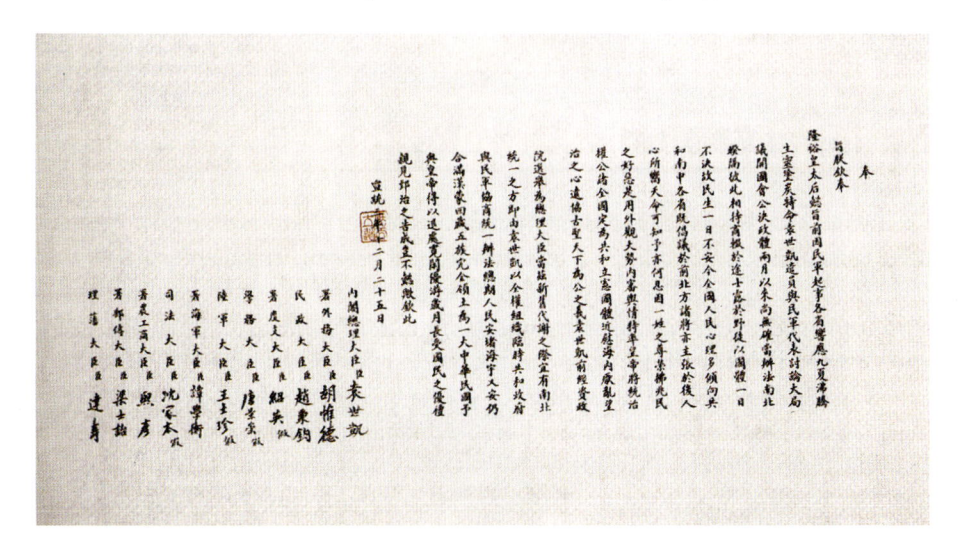

Abdication announcement of Emperor Puyi of the Qing Dynasty, February 12, 1912.

The site of the First National Congress of the CPC, held in Shanghai on July 23, 1921.

with the Chinese labor movement. The Communist Party of China (CPC) was founded in Shanghai in 1921, a milestone in the history of modern China. The CPC integrated Marxism with the actual conditions of China, contributed to the victory of the Anti-Japanese War, won the Liberation War, and founded the People's Republic of China on October 1, 1949.

National Capitalist Development

From the very beginning, China's national industry had two kinds: government-run industries dominated by the state and private capital enterprises.

The Anqing Interior Arsenal, the result of the Westernization Movement of the Qing imperial court, was established in 1861, the first for-profit, government-run enterprise. Prior to the 1870s, the Westernization Movement called for "self-renewal." A number of military factories were set up, including the Kiangnan Arsenal, the Fuzhou Ship-Building Bureau, and the Tianjin Manufacturing Bureau. After the 1870s, the Westernization Movement called out for "wealth," and a number of civilian-use factories were built, such as the Shanghai Merchants Steamship Bureau, the Kaiping Mining Bureau, the Shanghai Weaving Bureau, and Hanyang Iron Factory. These factories used

Kiangnan Arsenal, founded during the Westernization Movement.

advanced technologies and equipment, and their products were for both military and civilian use.

Government-run industry initiated by the Westernization Movement marked the beginning of Chinese industrialization and left a precious legacy for Chinese industrial, military, and educational departments.

Private enterprises emerged in the 1870s. Outstanding private companies were Shanghai Fachang Machinery Factory, Guangdong Jichanglong Filature Factory, and Tianjin Yilaimou Machinery Mill. After the Sino-Japanese War in 1894, the Qing imperial court loosened its restrictions on private factories and set up the ministry of commerce in 1903 to encourage industrial and commercial development. At that time, a campaign of saving the country through industry emerged in China, and a number of industrialists made contributions to the nation.

However, China encountered extreme difficulties in its effort to develop modern capitalism. Western powers tried to suppress China's national industrial development with their abundant capital, technological advantages,

China Cement Works in Nanjing, built during the Republican period, epitomizes China's early national industry.

and prerogatives they had gained in China. The high tax rate of the Qing Dynasty and extortion by governments at all levels increased the production costs, making China's national industries less competitive. Private enterprises had to rely on foreign capital to a certain extent, or seek protection from the domestic government for survival.

The founding of the Republic of China in 1912 raised the political status of the national bourgeoisie and inspired the enthusiasm of national capitalists to revitalize industry.

During World War I, major European countries were busy with the war, so capital and commodity exports to China were reduced, and Chinese national industry developed rapidly. From 1903 to 1908, the number of registered factories in China was 21 per year. The number increased to 41 between 1913 and 1915, and to 124 between 1916 and 1919. Soon after the end of World War I, foreign capital staged a comeback, putting Chinese national industry under heavy pressure.

In the 1930s, bureaucratic capital, as represented by the four large households (Chiang, Soong, Kung, and Chen), emerged prior to the Anti-Japanese War. Making use of their political rights, they obtained a great deal of resources and income by unified purchase and unified sale, monopoly sale, price

A spinning mill workshop in the Republican period.

restriction, and bargain measures. The four families took up a dominant position in national industry.

After the Opium War, Chinese people suffered from the resulting chaos and lowered living standards. During the period of the Republic of China, the limited social and economic development did not shake off their shackles of poverty. The purchasing power of the legal tender issued by the government of the Republic of China is a good example. Before the Anti-Japanese War, 100 yuan was worth two bulls. That same 100 yuan was worth two eggs in 1945, two pieces of coal in 1947, and only 0.0001 gram of rice in 1949. In the same year, China had 20,000 kilometers of railways, of which roughly half could be used. The length of useable highway was less than 80,000 kilometers, and most of the roads were located in the developed southeastern coastal areas. Highways were not available in mountainous regions or in border areas inhabited by ethnic groups, which made up more than two-thirds of the gross land area in the state. As a foreign commentator once said, China was a country that needed to import even an iron nail.

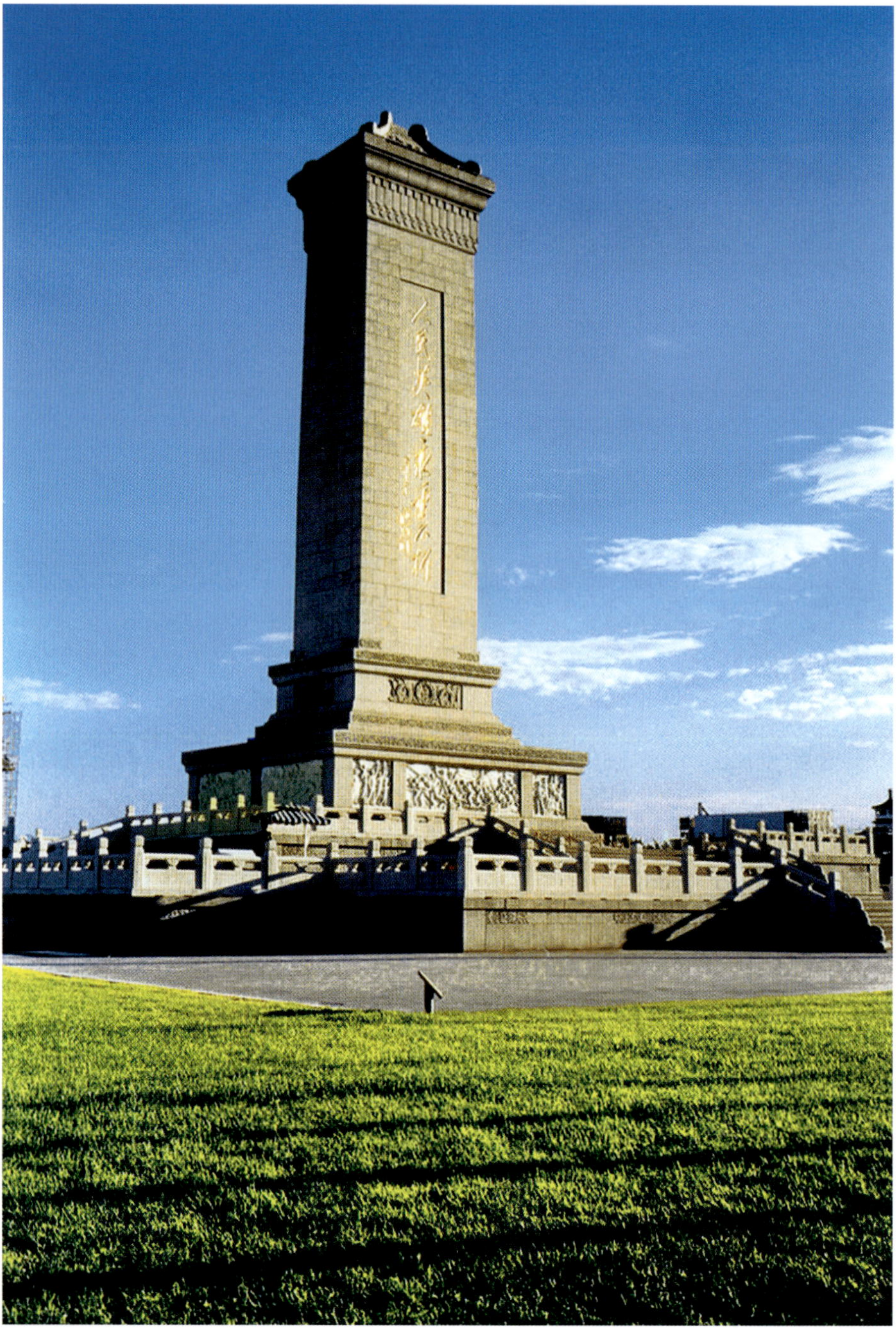

Chapter 10

The People's Republic of China: In Search of Socialist Modernization

On October 1, 1949, the People's Republic of China was founded. Over the past sixty years, China has been exploring its way toward socialist modernization through the introduction of democracy and legal systems in the political field, economic reforms, participation in international competition and cooperation, and the maintenance of world peace and stability.

Building up the Political System

Since its foundation, New China has dedicated itself to building a political system suitable for its practical conditions. The political system is composed of the people's congress, which operates by the principle of democratic centralism, multi-party cooperation and political consultation under the leadership of the Communist Party of China (CPC), and the system of regional autonomy of ethnic minorities.

The people's congress system is the fundamental political system of China. According to the Constitution of the People's Republic of China, the power of the nation belongs to the people. The National People's Congress and the local people's congresses at various levels, created by democratic elections, are the organs through which people exercise state power. They are responsible to the people and subject to their supervision. The National People's Congress, the supreme organ of state power, is entitled to amend the constitution, enact laws, elect national leaders, approve national economic development plans, and determine war and peace.

October 1, 1949 witnessed the founding of the People's Republic of China. Chairman Mao Zedong proclaims the Announcement of the Central People's Government on the Tian'anmen Rostrum.

Monument to the People's Heroes, Tian'anmen Square, Beijing.

Chapter 10 The People's Republic of China: In Search of Socialist Modernization   **191**

Celebrating the 60th anniversary of the founding of the People's Republic of China on October 1, 2009.

FYI FOR YOUR INFORMATION: THE HONG KONG AND MACAO TO CHINA

Hong Kong and Macao have been part of the Chinese territory since ancient times. Hong Kong was occupied by the United Kingdom after the Opium War; Macao was occupied by Portugal step by step after the mid-16th century.

The Chinese government formulated the policy of "One Country, Two Systems" to solve the Hong Kong and Macao issues left over by history. In December 1984, the Chinese and British governments signed The Joint Declaration on the Future of Hong Kong. In April 1987, the Chinese and Portuguese governments signed The Sino-Portuguese Joint Declaration on the Question of Macao.

The Chinese government resumed its exercise of sovereignty over Hong Kong on July 1, 1997, and over Macao on December 20, 1999. On these two days, special administrative regions were established, respectively, and the policies of "Hong Kong people administering Hong Kong," "Macao people administering Macao," and "a high degree of autonomy" have been implemented.

The system of multi-party cooperation and political negotiation under the leadership of the CPC is characteristic of modern China. The first constitution of New China formulated in 1954 stipulated the ruling party status of the CPC and the right of participation in the management of state affairs. In 1982, the CPC reiterated that it would work closely with democratic parties in the spirit of "long-term coexistence, mutual supervision, sincere treatment of each other, and the sharing of weal or woe."

The system of regional autonomy of ethnic minorities is implemented in response to the fact that China is a unified multi-ethnic country. China has fifty-six ethnic groups, and Han Chinese account for more than 90 percent of the gross population.

Over the years, people from various ethnic groups have come to inhabit some areas together, and some ethnic groups are centralized in other areas. Regional autonomy of ethnic groups is under the unified leadership of the state and aims at national unity and the equality of each ethnic group. Regional autonomy is implemented in some areas inhabited by ethnic people, and autonomous governments are established to exercise the right to autonomy. At present, China has five provincial-level autonomous regions and more than 100 autonomous prefectures and counties.

Since the 1980s, China has intensified its policy of political reform that aimed toward democracy and rule of law. In 1999, the tenet of "governing the country according to law" was added to the constitution, a milestone marking China's entry into a new historical stage of building a law-based society.

Socialist Economic Development

When the People's Republic of China was founded, all sectors of the economy required full-scale reconstruction. In 1953, the CPC determined the "general line during the transition period," with a view to realizing socialist industrialization and completing socialist transformation of the agriculture sector, the handicraft industry, and the capitalist industry and commerce in the long term.

In 1953, China began the implementation of the first five-year national economic development plan, whose goals were attained in advance in 1957. China built up such new sectors as aircraft, motors, electricity generation equipment, metallurgical equipment, and high-level smelting. Basic industries took shape. Iron and steel, and coal and power facilities were built in the central and western areas. A reasonable industrial layout emerged.

At the end of 1956, the socialist transformation of agriculture, the handicraft industry, and industry and commerce was completed, and a planned economic system was established. The system paved the way for the development of Chinese socialist industrialization and also exposed various defects of the system, foreshadowing later difficulties in economic development.

Due to underestimation of the arduous, complex, and long-term socialist construction process, Chinese economic development sought high speed in 1958. "Melting iron and steel," "people's commune," and "great leap forward" movements took place in China, upsetting the balance of the national economy, destroying the ecological environment, and dampening people's initiative for production.

Between 1956 and 1966, China's modernization drive experienced twists and turns, yet great achievements were made. An independent, large-scale industrial system was established. Power, mining, and machinery industries largely thrived. Electronic, nuclear power, and space industries emerged and grew fast. Large oilfields such as Daqing, Shengli, and Dagang were established. The railway linked all provinces, municipalities, and autonomous regions, except for Tibet.

From 1966 to 1976, China suffered the social turmoil caused by the Cultural Revolution. Grave mistakes in economic development almost destroyed the national economy, and seriously hindered China's industrial modernization. The Cultural Revolution brought a staggering economic loss of 500 billion yuan.

Farmers are filled with the joy of harvest after the implementation of the household contract responsibility system.

The Third Plenary Session of the Eleventh Central Committee of the CPC was convened in 1978. A decision was made to carry out reform and opening-up and shift the focus of the CPC's work to economic development, triggering a series of great economic reforms in China.

Reforms began in rural areas. The household contract responsibility system motivated farmers by setting farm output quotas for each household, allowing them autonomy in production and management. Township and village enterprises emerged and flourished, promoting rural development and improving the farmers' standard of living.

Reforms in rural areas drove the reforms in urban areas. In 1992, the 14th Central Committee of the CPC set the goal of restructuring the economic system, that is, establishing a socialist market-oriented economy by deepening the reform of state-owned enterprises (SOE), establishing modern corporate governance, and encouraging businesses to become legal entities and competitors. The SOE reform resulted in enhanced competitiveness and the rise of a number of dynamic, powerful, large enterprise groups. Some of these enterprise groups have now gone global.

During the SOE reform, some problems occurred, such as layoffs. As the social security system improves gradually, the situation will ease.

A street in Shenzhen, 1981.

Chapter 10 The People's Republic of China: In Search of Socialist Modernization

Today's Shenzhen.

While carrying on economic reforms, the Chinese government kick-started opening up as well. Since 1980, China has set up five special economic zones along its coastline and opened a host of coastal port cities, attracting foreign investments and developing export-oriented industries. In 1990, the central government decided to develop and open Pudong, Shanghai. By the 1990s, China had created an all-dimensional, multi-tiered, and wide-ranging pattern of opening up that encompasses both the eastern coastal and central and western inland areas.

China entered the World Trade Organization (WTO) in 2001, marking a new stage in its opening-up process. WTO membership has put the country in a better position to integrate itself into the international economic system.

Over the past three decades, reform and opening up have advanced each other and prompted China's fast economic growth. From 1979 to 2008, China's annual GDP growth rate was 9.8 percent, a rare phenomenon in world economic records.

Pudong, Shanghai, which has evolved from a rural area into a base of hi-tech and modern industries.

FYI — FOR YOUR INFORMATION

PROCESS OF CHINA'S OPENING UP TO THE OUTSIDE WORLD

Since 1978, China's opening up has undergone six phases: (1) trial establishment of special economic zones; (2) opening of coastal port cities; (3) further opening up of coastal areas; (4) opening and developing Shanghai's Pudong New Area; (5) all-around opening of cities along the Yangtze River and in border areas, and those of inland provincial capital cities; and (6) China's entry into WTO.

Over the past 30 years, China has successively set up five special economic zones, opened 14 coastal port cities and Pudong New Area in Shanghai, established 15 bonded areas, 32 economic and technological development zones, 52 high-tech development zones, and 38 export processing zones; and 13 border cities, 6 cities along the Yangtze River, and 18 provincial capitals.

According to World Bank statistics, the per-capita GDP of China was just US$230 in 1978, ranking 104th among the 126 countries and regions listed. At that time, many Chinese people did not have sufficient food or clothing. In 2008, China's GDP reached US$4.32 trillion, and China's economic aggregate was third in the world, with its per-capita GDP hitting US$3,266.

In 2002, the 16th CPC Central Committee called for the building of a well-off society in an all-around way and set a lofty objective of quadrupling China's GDP of 2000 by 2020 via optimized economic structure and enhanced profits.

Foreign Relations of Modern China

After World War II, the western and eastern campus confronted each other. As soon as the People's Republic of China was founded, the Chinese government started frequent diplomatic activities.

In terms of relations with neighboring and friendly countries, China proposed the Five Principles of Peaceful Coexistence, namely mutual respect for each other's sovereignty and territorial integrity, non-aggression, non-interference in each other's internal affairs, equality and mutual benefit, and peaceful coexistence. These principles, which were not bound by ideology or social system, were gradually recognized by the international community, and became

Chinese delegates are excited at the decision of the 26th General Assembly of United Nations to reinstate the legal seat of the People's Republic of China in October 1971.

In February 1972, US President Nixon visits China.

basic principles for conducting international relations. At the Bandung Conference of 1955, China advocated the guideline of "seeking common ground while reserving differences." The participants agreed on the Ten Principles on the basis of the Five Principles of Peaceful Coexistence, promoting unity and cooperation among Asian and African countries.

In 1971, the 26th General Assembly of the United Nations (UN) approved a proposal that recovered all legal rights of the People's Republic of China in the UN.

China–Japan Peace and Friendship Treaty is inked in Beijing, August 1978.

Chapter 10 The People's Republic of China: In Search of Socialist Modernization

Ping Pong diplomacy and the secret visit of Henry Kissinger to China in 1971 revived the Sino–US relations. US President Richard Nixon visited China in 1972, and both sides signed the Sino-US Joint Communiqué, emphasizing the conduction of Sino–US relations under the Five Principles of Peaceful Coexistence. In 1979, China and the United States established formal diplomatic relations.

Japanese Prime Minister Tanaka Kakuei visited China in 1972, and signed the Agreement of Normalized Relations between China and Japan, marking a new era in Sino–Japanese relations.

As relations between China and the US and Japan improved, many western countries established diplomatic relations with China.

Since the 1980s, China has continued to practice the Five Principles of Peaceful Coexistence. China did not ally with any big country or groups of countries. Rather it was committed to developing friendly and cooperative relations with all counties.

China has also contributed to regional peace and stability. In 1991, China joined APEC (Asia-Pacific Economic Cooperation). China signed the Foundation Declaration of the Shanghai Cooperation Organization with Russia, Kazakhstan, Kyrgyzstan, Tajikistan, and Uzbekistan in Shanghai, to establish the Shanghai Cooperation Organization. In addition, trade cooperation

China enters the WTO, marking its position as an important part of the global economic system, in December 2001

between China and the ASEAN countries developed in an all-around way, and the China–ASEAN free trade zone was established in 2001.

Since China recovered its lawful seat in the UN, the country has carried out activities in accordance with the objectives and principles of the UN Charter. As a permanent member of the UN Security Council, China actively takes part in peacekeeping actions and promotes the UN disarmament plan, making positive contributions to moderating the international situation and maintaining world peace.

By the end of 2009, China had established diplomatic relations with 171 countries, joined more than 100 inter-governmental organizations, and signed almost 300 international treaties. Today, China adheres to the principle of peace, development, and cooperation, practices an independent foreign policy of peace, follows a peaceful development approach, and implements an opening-up strategy of mutual benefit. China will continue to play a constructive role in international affairs and work toward a more reasonable and just international order.

In 2008, China hosted the 29th Olympic Games.

Appendix:

Chronological Table of the Chinese Dynasties

The Paleolithic Period	Circa 1,700,000–10,000 years ago
The Neolithic Age	Circa 10,000–4,000 years ago
Xia Dynasty	2070–1600 BC
Shang Dynasty	1600–1046 BC
Western Zhou Dynasty	1046–771 BC
Spring and Autumn Period	770–476 BC
Warring States Period	475–221 BC
Qin Dynasty	221–206 BC
Western Han Dynasty	206 BC–AD 8
Eastern Han Dynasty	25–220
Three Kingdoms	220–280
Western Jin Dynasty	266–316
Eastern Jin Dynasty	317–420
Northern and Southern Dynasties	420–589
Sui Dynasty	581–618
Tang Dynasty	618–907
Five Dynasties	907–960
Northern Song Dynasty	960–1127
Southern Song Dynasty	1127–1276
Yuan Dynasty	1271–1368
Ming Dynasty	1368–1644
Qing Dynasty	1636–1911
Republic of China	1912–1949
People's Republic of China	1949–present

INDEX

A
Art of War, 50, 84
Autonomous regions, 192–193

B
Banpo site, 5, 11–12
Bian Que, 42
Bronze, 13, 17–20, 23–28, 32, 35, 38–39, 41, 56, 66–67
Buddhism, 64, 88–89, 108, 159

C
Calligraphy, 83, 86, 89, 108, 114, 141, 170
Cao Cao, 77–78
Central government, 21, 55, 59–60, 102, 104, 120, 134, 150, 195
Central plains, 13, 15, 21, 32–34, 63–64, 81–85, 89, 93, 106–107, 119, 122, 124–125, 132–133, 160
Cheng-Zhu Neo-Confucianism, 139–140, 167–168
Chiyou tribe, 13
Chu, State of, 32–35, 37, 41, 43
Ci poetry, 140
Classic of Internal Medicine, 69
Communist Party of China (CPC), 184, 189, 192, 194, 197
Confucian philosophy, 48, 61
Confucius, 20, 40, 42–43, 45–46, 50, 72, 89, 167
Cultural Revolution, 193

D
Dalai Lama, 157–158
Democratic Revolution, 181–184
Ding, 20, 27–28, 32
Dujiangyan, 39, 41–42
Dunhuang, 62, 65, 86, 104, 106, 115–116

E
Economic reforms, 96–97, 189, 194–195
Erlitou Culture, 18, 24

F
Feudal system, 20–22, 33, 53, 138
Five Dynasties, 119
Five Principles of Peaceful Coexistence, 197–199
Four great inventions, 138–142

G
Genghis Khan, 132–133
Great Unification, 135
Great Wall, 53, 61–63, 154–155

H
Handicraft industry, 22, 192
Han Dynasty, 10, 48, 50, 58–69, 71, 73, 77, 79, 83, 89
Han Fei, 49
Hemudu Culture, 5, 7
Hongshan Culture, 5, 8–9
Huangdi, Yellow Emperor, 9, 69
Hundred Schools of Thought, 40–50, 71
Huns, 53, 61–63

I
Imperial examination, 100, 102–103, 108, 122, 129–130, 152, 166–167, 182

J
Japanese invasion, 181
Jiaguwen, 23–25
Jin Dynasty, 79, 82, 89–90, 92, 124–125
Jin, State of, 32, 34–35, 37
Jinwen, 24–25

203

K

Kangxi, 148–149, 155, 157
Kublai Khan, 132, 134
Kunqu Opera, 159, 170

L

Lao Tze, 44, 46–47, 50, 61, 71, 88
Legalism, 45, 47, 72, 88
Leninism, 183
Liao Dynasty, 122–123
Li Bai, 113

M

Manchu, 147–148, 157
Mao Zedong, 190
Materia Medica, 71
May Fourth Movement, 183
Mencius, 43, 45, 47, 167
Metaphysics, 88–89
Military Affairs Division, 149
Ming Dynasty, 63, 145–155, 157, 159–171, 173–174
Mogao Grottoes, 115–116
Mohist School, 45–47
Mongolian Empire, 132–133
Mo Tzu, 47

N

National People's Congress, 189
Neo-Confucianism, 139–141, 167–168, 173
Neolithic Period, 5, 11, 13
New Democracy, 192
Northern Dynasties, 77–93, 95, 101
Northern Song Dynasty, 121, 126–128, 136, 139, 141

O

Opening up, 194–196, 200
Opium War, 145–175, 177–178, 180–181, 187, 191

P

Paleolithic Period, 3
Patriarchal system, 21

Peking Man, 3–4
Peking Opera, 170–171
People's Republic of China, 184, 189–200
Porcelain, 5, 68, 100, 107, 122, 125, 127
Puyi, Emperor, 183

Q

Qianlong, Emperor, 149, 157–159, 163, 170, 175
Qin, State of, 34–39
Qi, State of, 32, 34–37, 49

R

Republic of China, 182–184, 186–187, 189–200
Revolution of 1911, 183

S

School of Eclectics, 45, 50
School of Mind, 140
School of Names, 45, 49
Sericulture, 11, 99, 133–134
Shang Dynasty, 18–19, 22–25, 27–28, 89
Shang Yang, 34–35, 37–39
Shen Nong, Emperor, 71
Shihuang, Emperor, 53–58, 61, 73–74
Silk Road, 64–65, 86, 107, 116, 135
Sima Qian, 72–73
Socialist Modernization, 189–200
Square-fields system, 23, 37
Sun Wu, 49–50
Sun Yat-Sen, 182–183

T

Taoism, 48, 72, 88–89
Terracotta Warriors, 39, 73–74
Three Kingdoms Period, 77–81, 93

U

Upper Cave Man, 3–6

W

Wang Xizhi, 89–90
Wang Zhaojun, 62
Wei, State of, 34–35, 37
Westernization Movement, 184–185

Western regions, 61–66, 79, 92–93, 105, 107, 109, 114, 121
WTO, 195–196, 199
Wudi, Emperor, 58–63, 65, 71–73

X

Xiandi, Emperor, 66, 78
Xixia, 119, 121–124, 136–137
Xuanzang, 109
Xuanzong, Emperor, 100, 106, 107, 113–114, 119
Xun Zi, 45, 47

Y

Yangdi, Emperor, 96–97
Yangshao Culture, 5, 12

Yan, State of, 34–35, 37, 45, 49, 61
Yin-Yang School, 45, 49, 72
Yuandi, Emperor, 62
Yuanmou Man, 3
Yu, chieftain, 121
Yue, State of, 33

Z

Zaju Opera, 140
Zhao, State of, 34–35, 37, 50, 61, 107
Zheng He, 173
Zheng, State of, 37
Zhuang Tzu, 46–48, 88